PRESSURE

True Stories by Teens About Stress

**Edited by Al Desetta
of Youth Communication**

free spirit
PUBLISHING®

Library of Congress Cataloging-in-Publication Data
Pressure : true stories by teens about stress / edited by Al Desetta.
      p. cm. — (Real teen voices)
  Includes index.
      ISBN 978-1-57542-412-5 — ISBN 1-57542-412-6 1. Stress in adolescence. 2. Stress management for teenagers. I. Desetta, Al.
  BF724.3.S86P74 2012
  155.5'189042—dc23

2012013824

eBook ISBN: 978-1-57542-656-3

Free Spirit Publishing does not have control over or assume responsibility for author or third-party websites and their content. At the time of this book's publication, all facts and figures cited within are the most current available. All telephone numbers, addresses, and website URLs are accurate and active; all publications, organizations, websites, and other resources exist as described in this book; and all have been verified as of May 2012. If you find an error or believe that a resource listed here is not as described, please contact Free Spirit Publishing. Parents, teachers, and other adults: We strongly urge you to monitor children's use of the Internet.

Photo credits from Dreamstime.com: cover © Scol22, p. 5 © Sangiorzboy, p. 12 © Milosluz, p. 17 © Ingrid Balabanova, p. 24 © Mashe, p. 30 © Antaratma Images, p. 37 © Felixcoinc, p. 44 © Sergey Peterman, p. 50 © Jameswimsel, p. 55 © Ingvald Kaldhussater, p. 61 © Anna Marie Nemcova, p. 72 © Finetti, p. 84 © Paul Hakimata, p. 89 © Yuri Arcurs, p. 97 © Nikolai Sorokin, p. 102 © Dmitrijs Dmitrijevs, p. 106 © David Gallaher, p. 111 © Kayx1984, p. 116 © Serban Enache, p. 127 © Jamie Wilson, p. 130 © Brighthorizons, p. 140 © Evolove, p. 143 © Justforever, p. 148 © Ghubonamin, p. 152 © Nicemonkey

Reading Level Grades 9 & up; Interest Level Ages 13 & up;
Fountas & Pinnell Guided Reading Level Z+

Cover and interior design by Tasha Kenyon

10 9 8 7 6 5 4 3 2
Printed in the United States of America
S18860413

Free Spirit Publishing Inc.
Minneapolis, MN
(612) 338-2068
help4kids@freespirit.com
www.freespirit.com

CONTENTS

INTRODUCTION

Family, friends, school, and relationships—while these can all be sources of support for teens, they can also lead to plenty of stress and conflict. In *Pressure*, teens describe how stress has affected them and what they're doing to lead more relaxed and healthy lives.

In "Enjoy the Moment," Ngan-Fong Huang has pushed herself relentlessly all her life to achieve academically. But by her senior year in high school, she begins to question her driven approach to life.

"Sometimes worrying too much just overwhelms me," she writes. "Last term, for instance, I went out of my mind over grades and college applications."

While it's important to plan for the future, Ngan-Fong also realizes that life is too stressful when she doesn't enjoy and value the present moment: "We should also spend time appreciating what is right before our eyes, since the present is what we have now."

In "House of Stress," the author is weighed down by taking on adult responsibilities in the family: "I sweep, clean the kitchen, and mop. When my stepsister doesn't help out, I clean the entire house alone." The author also has to babysit her disobedient siblings.

"I often feel frustrated and angry at the situation," she writes. "I don't want to be the kind of person who blows up, and I'm not, but that just leaves me feeling more frustrated."

The writer hopes that when she finally moves out of her house, she won't take all that frustration, anger, and stress with her. Rather, she hopes she takes away "the knowledge and ability to handle my responsibilities."

The stories in *Pressure* show teens engaging in a wide range of activities to release stress in healthy ways. One writer turns to Buddhist chanting to clear her mind. Janae Marsh finds calm and gains perspective by reading. Niya Wilson relaxes by doing yoga. Several others deal with personal problems through writing.

"I would open up completely in my diary," says one author. "It's almost like my head went from heavy to empty, especially when I wrote about my father's behavior. When I wrote my angry thoughts, my mind was less stressed. It's like I told someone my feelings and they offered to listen. I didn't feel sad or suicidal anymore."

Sports and exercise are a great help to other writers. Martin Smith plays basketball while D'nashia Jenkins runs track. Emily Orchier takes long walks.

The stories in this book offer a window into many teens' lives. You are sure to find within its pages people and experiences you can identify with and relate to.

You might find that you can get more out of the book by applying what the writers have learned to your own life. The teens who wrote these stories did so because they hope that telling their stories will help readers who are facing similar challenges. They want you to know that you are not alone, and that taking specific steps can help you manage or overcome very difficult situations. They've done their best to be clear about the actions that worked for them so you can see if they'll work for you. For further help, this book also features interviews with therapists and counselors about the causes of stress, how it affects people, how to identify it, and how to deal with it.

Another way to use the book is to develop your writing skills. Each teen in this book wrote 5 to 10 drafts of his or her story before it was published. If you read the stories closely you'll see that the teens work to include a beginning, a middle, and an end, along with good scenes, description, dialogue, and anecdotes (little stories). To improve your writing, take a look at how these writers construct their stories. Try some of their techniques in your own writing.

If you'd like more information about the writing program at Youth Communication or want to read more teen essays, visit www.youthcomm.org.

POETRY KEEPS ME CALM

by Ashunte Hunt

5

When I was 14, I was put in my first group home. I was facing many struggles at that time. I was still grieving for my parents, who had died when I was younger, and I was living with a stepmom who abused me. I also had to deal with bullying from my peers in middle school.

I was caught in a circle of abuse. I'd get beat up in school, and then I would go home and go through the beatings that my stepmom called "discipline." When I was put in the group home, I had to deal with a whole new situation all by myself, so I got really stressed out.

Not being able to express my feelings gave me no choice but to keep them bottled up inside, and the more I bottled up my feelings, the more likely I was to explode.

I had no way to express my feelings because I wouldn't talk to anybody. I didn't trust them. Not being able to express my feelings gave me no choice but to keep them bottled up inside, and the more I bottled up my feelings, the more likely I was to explode. My anger kept rising and rising, and then I'd get into fights or vandalize property. I always had evil thoughts in my head.

I looked at the world as if everybody was against me. I hated everyone I didn't know, and I grew very skeptical of the people I did know. And if I felt that I was being disrespected in any way, I just started spazzing like I was crazy.

I was my own Jekyll and Hyde—in certain situations I could control myself, but when someone provoked me I felt powerless to stop myself from going off on them. The people who pushed me to snap were the people who bullied me, made fun of my circumstances, and tried to play me like I was soft.

When I got mad in my group home, I turned into a demolition man. I demolished furniture, couches, chairs, walls, and my room. I also picked fights whenever people pushed my buttons.

One day in my group home the barber came through and I decided to get my hair cut. As I was waiting for my turn, I went downstairs and started playing a pinball game on the computer.

One of my peers came downstairs to tell me that it was my turn to get my hair cut. He tried to get me to go upstairs by turning off the computer screen. I turned it back on. I thought he was playing at first, so I didn't get mad or take it seriously.

He did it again and I turned it back on to continue playing. I started to get agitated. If my anger was a pot of water on the stove, it was just starting to bubble.

When he did it the third time, I turned it back on and told him, "If you turn off the computer screen again I will hurt you!" This time I was mad—the water was about to boil over.

Then he did it again. I was in a rage. We started fighting, we got a couple of hits in, then staff came to break it up.

I had so much anger in me at my group home that I didn't really want to deal with anything that anybody wanted me to do. But one day my favorite staff member let me listen to his Tupac and Eminem CDs. When I listened to Tupac and Eminem, I felt this unique feeling that no other artists gave me.

When I listened to Tupac's music, I got the message of street life and family problems. When I listened to Eminem's music, I felt the anger and rage that I'd been through. That's when the next stage opened up for me.

I was listening to one of Eminem's CDs and one song caught my attention. It was titled "Rock Bottom," and it was about how life can really push you to the edge and bring you down.

The first line pulled me in: "I feel like I'm walkin' a tightrope without a circus net." I related to that line because the lifestyle that I was going through made me feel like I was walking that tightrope. So I decided to write something of my own, and I got a piece of paper and a pencil.

In that first poem I expressed my built-up anger, rage, and depression. I didn't feel anything while I wrote it. But a week later I caught the feelings after reading it over and over again.

I called my first poem "Will somebody referee this fight I'm fighting?" One of the lines was: "I wouldn't care if the grim reaper reap, 'cause my life is something that I now don't want to keep." And that line alone hit me so hard that I had to dig into myself and see what would make me write that, because I really didn't recall writing it. That's when I realized how much pain I was in and how much I needed to release all my stress.

When I started to feel angry, I'd write a poem or two to release my feelings before I did something that I'd regret.

So I started writing more poetry. The poems that I wrote in my group home were about me, my anger, depression, stress, and any other thing that bothered me. When I wrote poetry it was like I could just write forever to express my feelings, as long as I had enough paper and lead to do so.

The poetry affected my anger a little at a time. When I started to feel angry, I'd write a poem or two to release my feelings before I did something that I'd regret. I'd still be angry, but I could at least let some of it out before it got out of hand.

When I found out that my first love had cheated on me, I wanted to chop her head off. Her love was priceless and I felt she threw my heart in the trash. I was so angry that I had to release my anger or I would have ended up in jail. So the first thing I did was write two poems. Then, when I saw her, I was able to stay calm even though it still hurt.

When I read over my poems I can acknowledge my feelings, and that helps me think about what I can do to make the situation better. I ask myself how I can do something different to avoid getting physical or making myself a threat to anybody.

I didn't get into that many fights after I started writing poetry, but I really can't say that it put an end to the fighting either. Sometimes I feel like going back to my old behaviors when I get mad because I still have a lot of anger inside of me. Certain situations give me flashbacks of how I would react if I were the old me.

I will still fight someone for disrespecting the memory of my mother and father, or for threatening me or my space. But it's been four or five months since I had my last fight.

And the last time I demolished something was a year ago. I was angry at my ex-girlfriend because we got into an argument over the phone, and I demolished my bowling trophy and some things that she had given me. I'll only demolish something now if I'm so upset that poetry can't help me.

Poetry can't help me get over the abuse I've been through or the fact that my parents are gone. I have to reach deep down inside to recover from those things, and even though poetry helps me get in touch with my inside, it doesn't cover those subjects. It might help numb it at times, but it doesn't hit the spot like I want it to.

But writing my feelings on paper taught me how to look at the world differently. My temper has calmed down, and I don't feel powerless over my behaviors anymore. I feel like a real human being who can civilize himself and cool off on his own.

My temper has calmed down, and I don't feel powerless over my behaviors anymore. I feel like a real human being who can civilize himself and cool off on his own.

ENJOY
THE
MOMENT

by Ngan-Fong Huang

Two friends and I were eating in a restaurant after school, and I happened to ask them what they wanted to become when they grew up.

"I don't know," one friend said, shrugging his shoulders.

"What do you mean?" I asked, surprised that he didn't seem to care. "Haven't you thought about the future yet?"

"There's plenty of time to decide later," the other friend added.

I couldn't believe how relaxed they were about the future, while I, on the other hand, never stopped worrying about completing tomorrow's "To-Do" list.

Then they asked me what my big plans were.

"Well, I have my life sort of planned out already. I want to become a doctor, so that means college, medical school, and then residency. That's about another 10 years of schooling for me. Later, I want to open my own clinic and probably do some laboratory research."

In the middle of our conversation, I suddenly remembered all the work waiting for me.

"Oh, no," I said out loud. "It's almost six o'clock, and I still have a calculus test tomorrow, an English paper due in a week, and a history presentation on Friday."

"Relax," they said. "Have some fun. This is senior year."

Throughout my life, I've always lived on schedules and "To-Do" lists. Often I feel guilty just sitting around. My motto has always been, "Time is money, so don't waste it."

I attend a high school where there's always a lot of academic pressure, so I've had to work hard in order to do well and I've pushed myself constantly.

Before going to sleep on a school night, I usually remind myself, "Remember to mail out the college applications," or "Start studying tomorrow for that killer physics test."

Other times I get down on myself for things I regret in my past. Sometimes worrying too much just overwhelms me and I become unhappy with my life. Last term, for instance, I went out of my mind over grades and college applications.

"What's wrong?" my friend Tiffany asked one day. "You seem so out of it."

"Just about everything's wrong," I mumbled. "No matter what I do and how hard I try, my grades are still dropping like fleas."

"Look," Tiffany tried to reassure me, "you're a smart girl and colleges see that. Anyway, you're going to study harder and do better on the next test."

"You're right," I said after hesitating for a moment. "That's exactly what I'm going to tell myself."

But all the memories I have of last term are depressing. I remember very few happy moments because I did not take the time to enjoy life for what it was.

So that's what I'm trying to do now, since I've already been accepted to college and I've got a little less stress in my life. Even though many of my friends and I talk about how we can't wait to go to college and how great it will be to live away from home, when we finally do go away we'll realize how much we miss our family, friends, and home.

We'll remember Mom's chicken with broccoli nostalgically. And when we're bored stiff in dull college towns, we'll say, "This city is dead. I wish it were more like New York."

We'll long for our youth, just like my grandmother, who always reminds me, "Back when I was young, all the boys would line up just to talk to me. My hair used to be long, black, and pretty. Now I'm old and my hair is all gray and short."

I'm not trying to say that we should live life enjoying only what is in the present. It's important to think about future plans and remember the past. If I hadn't, I might not be heading off to college this fall.

It's important to think about future plans and remember the past. But we should also spend time appreciating what is right before our eyes, since the present is what we have now.

But we should also spend time appreciating what is right before our eyes, since the present is what we have now.

This term I've been spending more time with my friends, and I'm happy to get to know them much better now. We go to the movies, eat out, chat, and, most importantly, we enjoy being together. A little voice inside my head still warns me about the work I need to do, but I don't let it overpower me anymore.

The other night a group of friends and I had just finished eating at a great diner in Manhattan and were walking toward the train station. The dark skies were clear, the breezes felt cool, and all I heard were the muffled sounds of cars driving past us.

I looked at the tall buildings around us, their glass windows reflecting the neon signs in stores. I held my head up high and really took a look at this beautiful city around me—a city I will be leaving in several months for college.

As I stood there enjoying the scenery and my friends who made the picture perfect, all I could think to myself was, "Wow, I haven't felt so happy in a long time."

It was at this moment that I let go of all my worries about grades, the future, and even the sadness of spending four years away from New York. I just brought my body and mind into the present and cherished that moment.

HOUSE
OF
STRESS

by Anonymous

The amount of stress in my house is overwhelming. My stepmother can't deal with her rambunctious kids, and too often she either yells at and hits them, or she just leaves the house and all the responsibilities to me.

My father works hard to support the family and pay the bills. He's a good dad when he's around, but he doesn't do much to change how my stepmother runs her household or treats their children.

Sometimes I feel so stressed that I want to scream or run away. But I don't, because I don't want to be the kind of person who can't handle my responsibilities.

As for me, sometimes I feel so stressed that I want to scream or run away. But I don't, because I don't want to be the kind of person who can't handle my responsibilities.

Instead, I take on many adult tasks. Sometimes I feel like the mother of the house.

Every weekend my stepsister and I are supposed to clean the house. I sweep, clean the kitchen, and mop. When my stepsister doesn't help out, I clean the entire house alone.

Then there's my three younger half-siblings, ages 4 to 10, to worry about. Most of the time, my stepmother can't handle them. My stepmother was once addicted to drugs and incapable of taking care of anyone. She beat her addiction about seven years ago, but it seems like she still has trouble dealing with all her responsibilities.

Sometimes my stepmother's nice. When no one gets to her, she speaks calmly, jokes around, and cleans the house. She has a good heart. But other times she scares me. She can be happy one moment, then in the blink of an eye she's screaming.

Any little thing can trigger her temper. If something bothers her too much, she gets angry at everyone in the house. Often she hits her children, too. When I see my stepmother hitting her children, it boosts my anger to high levels and I feel like calling children's services on her. I feel like hitting her.

My stepmother doesn't have a job. Sometimes she just lies down on her bed watching TV or sleeping. Other times she gets frustrated with the amount of work that needs to be done around the house and decides to go out. This generally happens several times a week. Usually I'm in my room doing homework when she comes in and tells me that she'll be right back.

She usually doesn't come right back, though. It's a routine. Usually she's gone for at least a couple of hours. Every time she leaves, I know that I have to get ready for the stress of watching my three little siblings. I'm so used to it now that I feel more resigned than bitter about it.

When my stepmother leaves, my stepsister, who's a year older than I am, usually just locks herself in our room and goes on the computer or plays a video game. I don't blame her. Because of her mother's addiction, she had to take care of the little ones while she was still very young herself. She had to grow up quickly, so I tell myself that she needs this time.

Still, sometimes I wish I wasn't the only one taking on all the responsibilities when my stepmother feels like she can't handle them. I often get the urge to lock myself in the room, too.

I don't, because I worry about the kids and feel like it's my duty to take care of them. I'm not sure why I feel like I should be responsible when other people aren't.

The result, though, is that I often feel frustrated and angry at the situation. I don't want to be the kind of person who blows up, and I'm not, but that just leaves me feeling more frustrated.

The most stressful part is when my little siblings don't listen to me.

"No" is my 4-year-old sister's favorite word. "Can you please stop jumping?" I ask her calmly, scared that she might slip or fall as she goes up and down on the couch. "NO!" she'll scream.

"Can you stop running down the hallway?" I ask her. "Can you be quiet? I'm trying to talk on the phone. Can you calm down?"

"NO! NO! NO!" is always her response. Sometimes I feel so frustrated that I want to scream.

I think my siblings feel like what I say isn't important since I don't punish them harshly or hit them like their mother does. I don't think children learn from being hit and I don't like seeing children in pain. I also don't want to be hitting my children when I have kids of my own.

Even so, sometimes I find myself yelling at my little siblings, and I've threatened them, too. I've told them, "I'm going to tell your mother, and you know what she's going to do if she finds out." I'm not proud of myself for using these tactics, but I also know that when I'm at the end of my rope threats usually work, because my siblings don't want to get beat.

The most stressful part is when my little siblings don't listen to me.

Things tend to be calmer when my dad's home from his job. My father has a lot to do because he's the one who pays all the bills for our family. He fixes things around the house, like leaky faucets and broken appliances.

When my dad's home, he's in charge. He also gets frustrated with the kids, but he doesn't hit them. Instead, he talks about what punishments they'll get if they don't listen, like not being allowed to go outside or play games. The kids know not to get on my dad's bad side because when he's mad, he screams and does the "I'm disappointed in you" thing.

My father has better ways of raising children than my stepmother. That makes me wonder why he doesn't do something to change how my stepmother raises her kids. But I haven't talked to my father about these things because I feel like I'd be adding to his burdens.

One of the most frustrating parts about living in my home is that, in many ways, my parents still treat me like a child even though I have adult responsibilities. My parents boss me around and remind me of the rules.

When I go out, they remind me what time I need to be home. They remind me to keep my grades up—even though my household duties often keep me from my schoolwork.

Sometimes I hang out with my friends. When I'm with them, I feel relaxed because I'm away from the stress at home.

It's unfair for them to treat me like I'm still a child. I take care of a lot in our house and I want them to treat me like the young adult that I am. It makes me determined to keep taking on those responsibilities, just to prove I'm grown up. But I feel like my parents don't respect me and that may be the most frustrating thing of all.

When I get frustrated, I usually don't express it. Instead, I walk to the park and think. I think about different ways to escape, like running away or moving away. I think about how much time I have left until I turn 18 and then graduate.

I go outside to read or write poems about how I feel. I often feel like I can't go on. I feel depressed and worn out. It's hard to feel frustrated all the time and not say anything about it.

Sometimes I hang out with my friends so that I don't have to think about it. Their company soothes me. We talk about everything that's on our minds and help each other out. When I'm with them, I feel relaxed because I'm away from the stress at home.

Even though I take on many responsibilities in my home right now, it helps to remember that my siblings aren't my children, and that soon I'll be able to escape and live my own life. I'll take on the responsibilities at home for now, but not for much longer.

I want to move out, but my father wants me to wait until I graduate. But I'm not even a senior yet, and I don't think I can wait that long. I'll just have to work up the courage to tell my dad that I want to move out sooner.

I hope that when I do move out, all the frustration, anger, and stress that I've experienced in my house doesn't come with me. I hope what I take with me is the knowledge and ability to handle my responsibilities. I believe these experiences have made me strong, and at least I have an idea of how to run a home. I hope that when I have my own family, I'll be able to discipline my children without so much anger and run a home without so much stress.

FORCED TO FACE COLLEGE

by Matt Lehrer

Today is the day my report card comes home. Unfortunately, it's sent home by mail. My mom doesn't trust me with the mail key since I have a habit of losing things. Plus she knows she'd never see my report card if I were allowed to pick it up.

I know she's gotten it when she says, "Matt! We need to talk."

Here it comes, the "I know you've been working really hard this quarter, but you need to step it up if you expect to get into a good college" speech.

"Okay, Mom," I reply, not really listening because I've had this talk too many times before.

Going to high school is stressful enough—the last thing I need is to think about college. But I hear it from my teachers, too: "Colleges like high grade point averages, so if you want to get into a good college, then you better work hard this year." At the Lab School, where I go, it's not only expected that you go to college, but that you go to a highly ranked college.

We started having assemblies in ninth grade to tell us what the school planned to do to prepare us for college. Sophomore year brought more assemblies, most of which reminded us to start thinking about college now.

The assemblies are supposed to make us familiar with the college application process, but they also succeeded in giving me panic attacks. They made it seem like colleges are watching my every move. If I mess up in physics this semester and colleges see my grades fall, then they'll be less interested in admitting me.

Each college seems to have different requirements. I need three SAT IIs to go to a school in California, but I'll need to take the Math B Regents to go to a school in New York, while a third school cares only about portfolios.

It makes me crazy because I don't know what school I want to go to and hearing all the requirements confuses me even more. I have enough worries about my physics test next week.

I'm being pressured on all sides to get A's so I can get into a good college, but I'm a B-average student. The A students get letters from the principals saying how proud they are that they keep such a high standard of excellence. All I get is a "you don't try hard enough" from my teachers.

Some people might say that being a B student is nothing to complain about. But I have high standards for myself and I don't do as well as I'd like. One problem is that I don't pay much attention to something if it doesn't interest me. I tend to do a halfhearted job on most of my homework and haven't studied nearly as much as I should.

My classes include advanced algebra, physics, U.S. history, computer programming, and English. With the exception of English, I have no interest in anything that I'm learning. Numbers hurt my head and I hate computers.

I usually like history, but with my (white American) history teacher going on about how hypocritical the U.S. government is or how evil white people are, all I'll get out of this class is a new self-loathing for being white.

I don't care for school and getting into college doesn't seem that important to me. But I can't help but feel that I may be wrong since everyone else is making such a big deal out of this.

> **When I think about college, I start to feel doomed. What if I can't get into a good college? Does that mean I won't get a good job?**

So I'm working harder than ever this year. I'm a junior, the year you have to be serious about your work because that's the year colleges look at most. But my grades don't reflect my efforts and it's frustrating. My teachers always tell me they know I can do better, but I'm starting to question that now. I'm actually trying this time and nothing has changed. I'm still stuck with that B, and an A average seems so impossibly far to reach.

When I think about college, I start to feel doomed. What if I can't get into a good college? Does that mean I won't get a good job? Am I going to be miserable for the rest of my life because I couldn't get an A?

In my chain of negative thinking, my SAT scores will be too low, we'll go to war somewhere, and I'll be drafted and get killed. I know it sounds crazy, but that's the way my mind works.

I get all panicky about getting into a "good college" when I'm not even sure that's the right fit for me. What others might consider a good college might not fit in with my plans for the future.

I want to be a music journalist when I grow up. I love listening to rock music and learning about its history. If there were a class on it, I'd take it in a heartbeat.

I've heard that some colleges offer courses on music history, so I'll look for those when I start applying. And I think I need to go to a school with an excellent journalism program or student newspaper, and do an internship with a music magazine. If I can fit college and music into the same category, I might feel more at ease in thinking about my future plans.

Listening to music is the only way I get away from the pressure I feel. I can listen to my stereo for hours on end, which helps me take my mind off of college.

In fact, listening to music is the only way I get away from the pressure I feel. I can listen to my stereo for hours on end, which helps me take my mind off of college. And playing guitar helps me relax as well. It's after I stop listening to and playing music that my stress comes back.

Part of the problem is that I just seem to be going along with the flow of whatever it is my parents want. I let them think about college for me since it makes me too nervous, yet I don't know if what they plan for me is what I want.

I haven't spoken to my parents about it because I feel like I'd be letting them down if I told them I can't handle something as simple as thinking about college. I feel like I've already disappointed them by not doing as well as they'd like me to in school.

If I felt I could talk to them, though, I'd tell them that I think it's too early to start thinking about college. I think I should wait until senior year, so we know where I stand and can narrow down school options without too much stress for me.

What I'd like to get out of college is something that helps prepare me for a career that works for me. I think I need to go somewhere that's going to allow me to choose my direction in life, rather than a place that's going to tell me that "all our students end up in accounting, so that's our plan for you." I need to be able to think for myself and figure out my future at my own pace.

YOGA RELAXES ME

by Niya Wilson

For a while, I was bummed out and I couldn't find a solution to my problems. My grades were slipping and my friends were truly being annoying.

I tried facing my problems head-on by actually going to class and telling my friends to shut up. I also tried putting my problems behind me by leaving my friends alone and avoiding them. None of that worked. Actually, it stressed me out even more.

Then my know-it-all friend told me about yoga. She said, "Yoga is the greatest way to relieve stress." Of course, being the Doubting Thomas that I am, I thought she was totally out of her mind.

She does her yoga exercises all the time, and she always does this chanting thing and massages her face in circular motions. I said to myself, "I couldn't be seen doing something like that."

How could being "one with myself" be healthy? It sounded crazy to me.

To try to get me involved in yoga, she said, "See how happy I am doing yoga? I'm more relaxed and stress-free. You could be, too!" She said it with every inch of her pride.

"Yeah, right," I said. How could being "one with myself" be healthy? It sounded crazy to me.

Her nagging and her pleading made me even more stressed. As you can see, I get stressed a lot! I'm such a baby when I don't get my way. But I finally gave in and did some yoga exercises with her and, truthfully, I liked it a lot.

This is what we did. First, my friend lit scented candles to give the room a peaceful atmosphere. Second, I sat cross-legged on the floor and took deep breaths to clear my mind of all thoughts. Clearing my head was kind of hard, since everything my life depended on was on my mind. But I sat in silence and relaxed, and that made it all clear.

> **I realized that I was making my problems bigger than they were. I also knew my attitude had to change.**

While sitting in silence, I stretched a little to make my body as relaxed as my mind. Eventually, I couldn't think of anything.

Then, before I left this new relaxed world, I prayed—not only for myself, but for my family and friends (and even a few enemies).

After I opened my eyes I felt much calmer and I thought through my problems again. I realized that I was making my problems bigger than they were. I also knew my attitude had to change and that I had to start to get to know who I was and keep myself from doing things that I knew were not me.

I really liked the calm feeling of doing yoga with my friend and I got more curious about it. So when my teacher gave me a flyer for a local yoga center, I decided that I wanted to take a professional yoga class.

The night before the big class I was excited and a little nervous. I had butterflies in my stomach. I wasn't sure what to expect.

It took me a while to figure out exactly where the place was, but I left home so early that I got there when it was still closed. Class started at 9:45 a.m. and I was there at 8:21. While waiting for the doors to open, I tried to imagine what was inside.

I visualized a big room with candles and encouraging posters and pictures on the walls. I imagined massage tables and a teacher with a very soft voice. She would walk very gracefully, like she could just glide through the world.

I woke up to reality when the doors opened. The place wasn't what I expected. It was small and very plain, with a black sheet covering the front entrance to block out any Peeping Toms who wanted to be nosy. There weren't any massage tables or posters and pictures around. I laughed at my imagination.

The teacher wasn't what I had imagined her to be, either. She was loud and stomped when she walked. When I introduced myself to her, she was cheerful, bubbly, and very nice. Because I couldn't do any exercises in my street clothes, I went to the bathroom to change into sweats.

When I walked out of the bathroom, the door to the main room was locked. I began to bang on it. Not one soul heard me, and I was getting mad until the teacher said, "Where's Niya? Oh, my, the door must have locked on her."

When she opened the door, my embarrassment grew as I stepped into the room and the other yoga students, all adults, were staring at me.

The class began. I had no idea what I was doing, so I copied what I saw. I picked up a mat and placed it on the floor. I sat on the mat and the teacher said some words in a totally different language. Then she told us to sit cross-legged, close our eyes, and repeat after her. She continued in a chant.

To me, it seemed really weird to be chanting. I felt like I was in a cult where everyone did the same thing, the same way. After the chant, there was complete silence for maybe one minute. I couldn't help but open my eyes and glance at the other students. They were all perfectly still. They looked as though they already had taken this beginners' course. The teacher spoke again, so I quickly closed my eyes.

She instructed us to go get a belt (really, a long piece of thick fabric) and said, "Put the belt over your shoulder." I totally thought this was weird. I had to put my right arm over my right shoulder, and my left arm under my left shoulder, holding the belt behind my back.

The teacher said a lot of strange phrases like, "Let your face feel like butter," and, though weird, they helped me relax.

Holding this position, I had to push my chest up, stretching my front and back muscles. After standing in position for a moment (it was hard!), the teacher told us to exhale out of the stretch.

During this exercise, the teacher said a lot of strange phrases like,

"Let your face feel like butter," and, "Stretch your body like a playful cat that has just woken up to a warm glass of milk." To me her phrases were humorous, and though weird, they helped me relax.

The rest of the exercises were pretty much the same: stretching and breathing. It sounds simple, but the way we had to hold the positions was really hard and, by the end, my muscles hurt.

My favorite exercise was the very last one. We each lay on top of a blanket that had two blankets on top supporting our heads. I also had a round pillow for my back. I lay completely still with my chest sticking out. The teacher told us to close our eyes and "be one with ourselves."

While I was lying there the teacher put a blanket over me (well, not just me, but the entire class). Her next instructions were to "relax and take everything off your mind. Concentrate on yourself, nothing else."

She continued to say this until I drifted off. I didn't think I was asleep because I still heard her talking, but I felt like I was in my own world.

When the class was over, I felt kind of tired and calm. It was a little strange, but I liked it.

In the beginning, I was definitely skeptical. Giving yoga a chance made me see how taking time to stretch and relax could give me a new way to handle stress. It gave me quiet time to be with myself and God.

Like me, most teens are faced with many stressful sit-uations, and we don't know how to go about dealing with stress. So we settle for not handling the situation or for handling it without thinking of the consequences. Yoga is something to try—it can calm you and clear your head.

MY
JOURNAL
SAVED
MY LIFE

by Anonymous

When I was in the ninth grade, my mom lost her job and we didn't have any money to keep our apartment. My dad had left us and wasn't giving us financial support. I was really depressed (you can imagine how my mom felt) because I was concerned about my next meal and where I would sleep.

I wasn't really talking to anyone about what I was going through, which wasn't a good feeling. But because of all the stuff that was happening to me, I eventually started keeping a journal, which really helped me out. I gained a better understanding of myself and how to handle emotional problems through writing in and re-reading my diary.

> **Writing allows my emotions to pour out of my emotional storage bag, my heart. Once it's opened and my feelings are released, I feel at ease.**

Writing allows my emotions to pour out of my emotional storage bag, my heart. Once it's opened and my feelings are released, I feel at ease.

But when I'm going through a hard situation and my emotional storage bag is closed, I feel a lot of pressure. I worry that I may eventually explode or take out my pain on someone else if the pressure is not released.

At one point, my father was the main source of that pressure. He made everything a nightmare for me. He was physically abusive to my mother when they lived together. Even though I wasn't the one who was getting abused, I hated him for hurting her.

Sometimes I wished he would die. But those were just angry thoughts. I didn't really mean it. I always thought that I should try to forgive him because he was my father and it was the "Christ-like" thing to do.

I felt like I was basically on "No-Man's Island." I had just started high school and was getting to know people there. I couldn't talk with my friends about what was going on at home. I didn't feel like I could trust anyone. I felt pushed into isolation.

Sometimes my father still slept at our house. But toward the end of the school year, he stopped helping my mom with the rent. She couldn't afford the apartment alone, so the landlord told us we had to move if we couldn't pay.

We moved to a two-room basement apartment about two or three blocks from where we used to live. It was small and I didn't like it, but it was the only thing we could afford.

Apart from getting good grades, nothing in my life was good. I felt suicidal. I wanted God to take me. Life to me was just not worth living because everything was so complicated, and at 14, I just couldn't understand why I had to deal with so much.

I made it through ninth grade, even though I felt terrible. My father was still calling my mother even though they weren't living together. On one particular summer night, he called and they got into a heated conversation. He threatened to kill her.

I think my mother was worried, but she didn't show it. I felt horrible. The thought of losing my mother terrified me. This is the event that caused me to write in my diary for the very first time. It was really just a plain notebook, but I felt like I had to write in it. I had to release what I was feeling.

When I began to write in my journal, I was finally able to detail what was happening with my parents. Although my diary couldn't offer advice, it was such a relief to get my emotions down on paper.

I began to write in my journal almost every day. After I poured out everything in those entries I felt much better, even though I was still worried about what would happen to my mother.

Sometimes I wished he would die. But those were just angry thoughts. I didn't really mean it. I always thought that I should try to forgive him because he was my father.

I would open up completely in my diary. It's almost like my head went from heavy to empty, especially when I wrote about my father's behavior. When I wrote my angry thoughts, my mind was less stressed. It's like I told someone my feelings and they offered to listen. I didn't feel sad or suicidal anymore.

Eventually I realized that writing was helping me cope with my father. Actually, I think my diary saved me. Whenever something happened pertaining to my father's behavior, I would write it down. Before I had my diary, I would just sit and cry and hope for the best when something bad happened. Sometimes I prayed, too. But writing helped me the most.

A few days after making an entry, I would go back to read what I wrote. Re-reading the journal entries still made me angry as I remembered those awful situations, but the feelings of hate toward my father had left me.

Thankfully, my home life eventually got better. My mother got a job and we were able to start getting back on our feet. She said that as soon as she got enough money, we would move to a better apartment.

My dad is now incarcerated because of other offenses, so I don't fear him hurting my mom anymore. We correspond with him by mail. (We don't know when he'll be let out.)

My journal helped me let go, and as a result, I've changed a lot. I understand myself better now. I've also been able to write about things besides my difficult home life. After reading my diary a few times, I noticed that I write about sports a lot. As a result, I decided to get involved in some sort of athletic activity, and eventually joined a couple of sports teams in high school.

I've also written a lot about boys. I've kept a record of the guys I dated and how I felt about them. Reading these entries now, I realize that for a long time I was looking for a father figure, not a boyfriend.

I noticed how the guys I would go for were usually older and more serious. I felt like I always wanted a guy who could give me fatherly advice as well as intimacy, probably because I lacked a father who was consistent in my life. I didn't feel like my dad loved me since he was hurting my mother.

But I see things a lot differently now. Re-reading my journal entries, I realize that I'm a capable person and I don't need a boyfriend who would be like a second father.

For instance, in one of my entries, I wrote about Ron. He was definitely a father figure, but I realized I never liked how I felt around him. I didn't feel I could fully voice my opinion around him because he had a serious, gruff tone that scared me. Scanning my entries on Ron, I began to figure out that I may be better off dating a guy who could be a boyfriend and a friend at the same time, a person who isn't always serious.

Sometimes I want a boyfriend who is more vibrant and has a childish side, and is not a stern authoritarian. My journal helped me figure out that I wanted someone to have fun with. Nothing serious!

My journal was my best friend. It made me think and helped me come up with different ways to handle problems by myself.

I still write in it, but I feel more comfortable now talking about my problems with a few chosen friends. My diary has made that a lot easier as well. By writing down how I feel about something before talking about it, I'm a lot clearer about what I want to say. I don't have to hustle to figure out my feelings right before I speak.

I now have over three years of my life recorded in a book. I'm so glad to have my journal. I recently named it "Precious," because that's how I feel about all the thoughts it contains.

STRESSED
FOR
SUCCESS

by SaeRom Park

It isn't easy to return to school after vacation and a week of adequate sleep.

I think of the nights when I felt like punching out the blinking computer screen after staying alive on tea and carbonated drinks. I can just feel my clammy hands when I recall those Mondays when I had three tests in a row. Those Sunday nights were even worse.

School is starting again and so is the race to the top where only the superhuman teens with perfect GPAs, high SAT scores, and 20 extracurriculars will survive. Well, that's what it seems like, anyway.

> "It's never too early to start thinking about college." These words have often crept into my nightmares as I sleep through a torrent of SAT words and college applications.

I'm a sophomore, and many juniors and seniors tell me, "It's never too early to start thinking about college." These words have often crept into my nightmares as I sleep through a torrent of SAT words and college applications.

I actually had a horrible dream that I couldn't get into any of the colleges I applied to. I woke up in a sweat, feeling like it was already too late to do anything about my future.

I go to Hunter High School, a specialized school. There are a lot of things that are really great about Hunter, including the fact that there are only about 200 people in my grade and it's easy to get to know almost everybody. Plus the quality of our education is good.

But about every two months, all the teachers simulta-
neously give "hell week" and we are loaded with assign-
ments, projects, tests, term papers, and essays from six
or seven different classes.

At times like these, I seriously feel like crawling under
my blanket, falling asleep, and never, ever coming out. I
think to myself, "Is this healthy?"

My friend Judy, 15, also a sophomore at Hunter, agrees
that stress is, by all means, a way of life. She slaves away
for three and a half hours a night on mindless homework so she can go to the college of her choice. She's
afraid that if she doesn't, she'll be lost.

In addition, Judy gets a lot of pressure from her family.

"My parents are the first generation in America," she
said, "and we're not doing so well." She explained that
because her parents couldn't really speak English and
knew only Chinese customs, it was hard for them to get
good jobs.

"Now my parents pressure me to work harder than
the next person," she said, "because I have to do better
just to be where everyone else is."

But while Judy and I have both been stressing over
our huge workload, I know other teens face a different
kind of academic stress.

Baudilio, 15, used to attend Smith Vocational High
School in the Bronx but transferred out.

Baudilio aspires to be a writer, but he said he doesn't know of any advanced placement or accelerated classes in his school, and he wasn't getting the kind of education that he wanted.

He guessed that only 3 out of 10 of his friends would graduate from high school. No one seemed to care about school, least of all his friends. "They talked about everything except academics," he said.

Each night during the school year, Judy and I plow through hours of homework. When I asked Baudilio how long it took him to finish his homework, he grinned and answered, "At least three seconds . . . in all."

Baudilio felt that if he failed, it wouldn't matter that much because he would become "just another story." But Baudilio also didn't want to fail.

When Baudilio was studying to take the entrance exam to get into Bronx Science High School, he said stress "used to overpower me . . . I actually fell ill with a headache. I had a fever and became really sick because I was trying so hard."

Unfortunately, Baudilio didn't make it into Bronx Science, but he applied to Urban Academy, an alternative high school located in Manhattan. He knew that if he stayed at his old school, he wouldn't have opportunities to pursue a career in writing.

Even though Baudilio's experience at school has been so different from mine, talking to him made me see that we were both stressed because we both cared about our futures.

Just out of curiosity, I asked Baudilio to tell me one wish that would make all his stress go away. He replied, "I want to be fearless." Tests, colleges, and interviews all make him nervous, and he just wants to be able to face them.

I thought, "Wow, that's what we should all be—fearless."

We need to remember that we're not supposed to be perfect, and that failing a test or even a class doesn't mean that we'll never achieve our goals in life.

Before I wrote this story, I knew that I wasn't the only student in this world who had academic stress, but I didn't know anything about how others experienced it or why students put up with it.

I was surprised when I found that most of the teens I talked to said they felt like they had no choice but to deal with the stress. We're stressed because, in one way or another, we're motivated to do well and because we have goals that we want to achieve.

But we should also know what our priorities are—no matter what, our own well-being and health should come first. There are times when academics are just not worth the stress, or when stress may get to be too much for some of us. We need to remember that we're not supposed to be perfect, and that failing a test or even a class doesn't mean that we'll never achieve our goals in life.

Still, we choose to face stress every day because we have a place we want to go, a somebody we want to be.

I know now that the next time I feel like crawling under the blankets and never, ever coming out, well . . . I'll lie there for five minutes, max. Then I'll face that stupid computer and start typing again.

BOOKS
GOT MY
BACK

by Janae Marsh

50

I love to read. For as long as I can remember, all I did was read. If somebody wanted to see me, they knew where to find me: on my bedroom floor with my Pocahontas blanket, reading any book I could get my hands on.

Reading was my escape from the world. To this day, when I'm reading, I don't know what's going on around me. And when I feel like my problems are too big to handle, reading helps me calm down.

My mom died when I was 2 years old and I ended up living with my grandmother and my aunt. Reading came in handy when my aunt and I were not getting along.

My aunt could be really hostile. She would call me dumb and stupid, and tried to make it seem like I was the devil in disguise.

One day I was in the living room watching cartoons. A character with a nasty attitude was on the screen. My aunt came over and said, "That little girl reminds me of somebody I know." She said that I acted just like the character—good around important people, bad around her and Grandma. But I didn't think that was true.

Reading was my escape from the world.

Sometimes she'd walk around the house, her eyes at me or my cousins for no reason. I'd be like, "Grandma, I ain't say nothing to her," but my grandmother wouldn't say anything. I felt powerless because I was this skinny little child who nobody listened to. It made me sad, too, because it seemed like my grandmother didn't care.

At times like that, I tried not to let what they said stick in my mind. I'd think to myself, "She's unhappy and misery loves company." But whenever my aunt or grandma would start talking about me or calling me a problem child, I'd take my Pocahontas blanket and my Goosebumps books and lock myself in the bathroom. I would sit in the bathtub, close the shower curtain, and read for hours. The bathtub was my getaway without having to run away from home.

When I feel like my problems are too big to handle, reading helps me calm down. If you walk in my house and you see me reading, I'm probably mad and trying to calm down.

The longer my aunt and I argued, the longer I stayed in the bathroom. Avoiding the situation did work, because eventually my aunt left me alone.

But it did get so bad that one time my brother had to go to his friend's house to use the bathroom. His friends would say, "Yo, Phil, it's all right if you're an only child." He was like, "I do have a sister. She's reading in the bathtub."

My grandma would try to lure me out. In the summer- time she always kept frozen treats in the freezer for me. My grandma also got me a television because I couldn't go to sleep unless I stayed up at night watching cartoons. The day I got a television, my brother got so mad! He was like, "Why'd you get her that? She's not gonna watch it! She won't even know it's there!" He came in my room to watch TV during the day, while I was still reading in the tub.

Reading didn't just help me escape, though. I think it made me smarter and more thoughtful. Reading helped me relax and gave me time to calm down before I confronted a problem.

In my house there are lots of children, and they all drive me up the wall. Sometimes I just want to be alone. So when they start acting up, I grab a book before I slap one of them. If you walk in my house and you see me reading, I'm probably mad and trying to calm down.

Reading helps me get perspective on my life. When I was younger, I always thought about how life would be different if my mom were around. My life wasn't really rough, but it was hard dealing with her death when I was so young. As I got older I couldn't really remember my mom, and I guess that's what made it so hard.

When I read A Child Called It, about a boy who was terribly abused, I was thinking, "Here's this little boy whose mother is beating him for no reason." I always knew that awful things happened to others, too. But after reading A Child Called It, my views about my childhood changed.

I thought that my grandma was so mean, but no matter how mad she got she never tried to burn me or hit me. And she would never call me "it." The book taught me to think about others even though I have my own issues.

I also like how reading lets me put myself in other people's shoes. Most recently I've read the Harry Potter series. I like fantasy books because sometimes I don't want to be Janae. I want to be Winter, the ghetto princess in Sister Souljah's book *The Coldest Winter Ever,* or Addy, the hero of a series called Addy: An American Girl.

Addy is my favorite because she is so brave. Addy went through being a slave, having her father and brother taken away from her, and having to leave her baby sister. Addy and her mother also had to run away to Philadelphia.

Often, if you grow up knowing one way of living, you're not going to try to change it because many people don't like to change. That's why I like Addy. What 9-year-old do you know who could go through all that and stay positive? She's like a role model to me.

For a long time, reading helped me understand myself and the world around me, even when I had no one to express myself to. Luckily, I've finally found someone who understands me. She's my cousin Maddy. When we were younger, we always played together and kept each other company. Now we are very close. I see her almost every weekend. If she comes over, I'll get out of the bathroom and we'll talk.

But during the week, my cousin isn't here. So when I need to step back from life, I always have my books.

RUNNING MY PROBLEMS AWAY

by D'nashia Jenkins

On a Saturday morning last November, I had to get up at 5 to be at the Armory track on 168th Street in Harlem, a neighborhood in Manhattan. I live in Coney Island, another New York City neighborhood more than an hour away.

At 5 a.m. my body didn't want to move. But my coach and the team were counting on me, and I didn't want to let them down. I was going to do the long jump and run the 4 x 2 sprint medley, a relay race with four runners.

I was excited because I love doing relays, especially at the Armory. It's a huge building that takes up a whole block and holds 3,000 people. A lot of famous runners, like Marion Jones, raced at the Armory.

Going there made me feel like a big-time runner. My first time at the Armory I didn't think I could run in front of all those people, but I did. After every race, I felt more comfortable.

I put on my uniform: a blue shirt that says "Abraham Lincoln" with the number 557, blue shorts, and shoes. As I got dressed, I felt proud of myself and the team.

I joined the team when I was a freshman at Abraham Lincoln High School. I hadn't considered it until a girl came up to me and said, "You look like a good runner. Would you like to join the track team?"

She thought I would make a good runner because she saw that my legs and arms were built. She thought I already ran track, but I didn't. I'm just naturally lean.

I was excited and surprised. "I don't know," I said. "What do I have to do?"

She answered, "It is a lot of hard work and dedication. It's not easy."

She was right. My team had practice every day from 3:30 to 6 except for Fridays. When we didn't have practice or a meet, I'd run on my own on the boardwalk. I got faster and faster.

Track helped me get away from my troubles. Arguments with my mom, problems with schoolwork, and drama with the kids at school all made me stressed. Running helped me take some of the worry away, and I felt better after every race.

I felt emotionally stable when I ran because it was the one thing I could control in my life. I made the choice whether I was going to run my best, run poorly, or not run at all.

I felt emotionally stable when I ran because it was the one thing I could control in my life. I made the choice whether I was going to run my best, run poorly, or not run at all.

If I didn't do well in a race, it was because of me. If I did well, I was able to say, "I did it on my own. I worked hard, and I won the race for me and not for anyone else."

That's what I was hoping for that morning in November—to do well. It was still dark outside when I met up with some of my teammates at the train station.

We got to the Armory at 7 a.m. and went to the second floor where the athletes work out and warm up before their races. Half of the team was already there, including the coach. They were all excited to see me, saying, "Hi, Nay Nay." I gave them hugs and high fives.

I had to wait two hours before my race started, so I read a novel (for fun, not school), listened to music, and talked with my teammates. At this point I was relaxed.

But when the officials called for the 4 x 2 girls sprint medley, I was suddenly so nervous that I was actually shaking. I jumped up and down to calm down. I told myself, "Nay Nay, you can do this."

We had to go downstairs to the waiting area by the track. I shook my legs, hands, and arms and stretched. We stretched together as a team, then we huddled together in a circle, putting our arms around each other, and encouraged one another to do our best.

"It's just another race at the Armory," I said to myself, but I still couldn't get rid of my butterflies.

They called my race again, and I went out to the starting line. I could hear the crowd rooting for different teams. As I stood at the line, I could feel the energy of the other runners.

I felt like all eyes were on me. It was like playing a basketball game, when one shot could send your team to the playoffs. The crowd is screaming "defense, defense," and you hear a loud roar and the buzzer goes off.

That's exactly how I felt, except I was standing in a lane next to five other runners waiting for the gun to go off to start the race. (No, it wasn't a real gun—no bullets, just a loud bang and smoke.)

I brought all my problems to the line. I thought about all the pain I felt inside, the worries and stress. I worried about passing my classes, about finals and exams that were coming up in school.

I was stressed about my mom's rules. She hadn't wanted me to come to the Armory because she didn't want me to walk to the train that early by myself, and we'd argued about it.

I was focusing so much on myself, I started to forget about the crowd. This is usually what I did at races.

Then the gun went off. I started running away from my problems. I thought, "My mom gets on my nerves. She doesn't understand me," and, "I just know I'm not going to pass math class if I don't pass the final." But these worries went away as I pounded the track. I was running my pain and hurt off my back.

I wasn't only fighting against my opponents, I was also fighting to win my battle against stress at school and home.

I couldn't see anyone or anything but the finish line. Everything else was just a blur. I fought to get to the finish line. I wasn't only fighting against my opponents,

I was also fighting to win my battle against stress at school and home.

I could feel the wind blowing against my skin. I felt like I was flying. My stress had disappeared.

As I approached the finish line, I could see the officials and the Armory's photographer ready to snap my picture. People in the stands looked like they were jumping out of their seats in slow motion.

I could see other runners on the side screaming, but I couldn't hear anything but my rapid breathing.

Then, as I crossed the finish line, I heard everyone screaming and everything went back to normal speed. I came in second as I passed the baton to my teammate. I felt proud of myself.

I hopped off the track and looked back at the problems that I left behind. I couldn't see anything, but I knew they were still there. Still, I felt better about them because I took care of them my way—by running them off. I felt like the weights I'd been carrying were lifted off my shoulders.

I fell to the floor, but my teammate pulled me up so that I wouldn't tighten up or get cramps. "Come on, Nay Nay, get up and walk it off," Simone said. She extended her arm to me, and I grabbed her hand and pulled myself up.

Then we joined the rest of the team, and they said, "Good job, Nay Nay." I looked at my coach and asked him how I did. "You did great. You should be proud of yourself."

And I was.

TEARS OF A CLOWN

by Eugene Han

Most people who know me would be surprised to hear that I've struggled with loneliness and depression for much of my life.

I'm always the guy who cracks a joke or adds sarcastic side comments to lighten up any conversation. I never have anything sad to say and I always try to bring people into the conversation so they won't feel left out.

But a deeper, more meaningful me exists. I've dealt with a lot of serious issues in my life—the absence of a family member, failure in school, financial instability, and coming to terms with my sexuality. I may be silly and social in public, but I act this way because I don't like it when people pity me. It makes me feel sorry for myself, so I just cover all my problems.

Maybe it started when my mother was arrested on a drug charge and sent to prison when I was only 7.

I believe my mother was unjustly sentenced. While she did have a connection to a big dealer, she personally didn't deal drugs. Why didn't the courts ever consider that she was a single parent with two young children? I felt anger, sadness, and frustration. It was as if they were ripping away the only support I had without a second thought. (My father had left us when I was a year old. He's never helped my family, ever.)

Before she went to jail, my mother asked my great-grandmother to move in and look after us. She did cook for us, but other than that she just sat around and watched TV. She was very old, illiterate, and crippled (she had broken her hip and had trouble walking). I always wished she wasn't handicapped, that she could have done more with us, taken us places. It was up to me to take on responsibilities normally taken care of by an adult. It became my job to pay bills, read, and translate important letters—even though I was still a little kid.

To make matters worse, when I was in school, kids would call me f— at times. (I guess they thought I was feminine or something.) I would cry every night, staring up at the stars from my bedroom window, just wishing and hoping that my mom would return the next day. As the years passed, her return felt more and more like an impossibility. It seemed useless to keep hoping. I felt my heart ache and sink deep within me.

> **It was up to me to take on responsibilities normally taken care of by an adult. It became my job to pay bills, read, and translate important letters—even though I was still a little kid.**

I tried burying myself in my schoolwork and reading lots of books, especially mysteries, so that I wouldn't have to think too much about it all. At home, I only had my brother, and we've never been tight. We're total opposites. He did nothing to help out the family, which made me feel even more alone in my efforts. At school, I mainly kept to myself. I was never popular and I never hung out with anyone in particular. I was more of a homebody, and my responsibilities kept me busy.

When I was 14, I started feeling down and lost interest in things—especially school. I felt too tired to get out of bed, and more than ever before I felt overwhelmingly lonely. That year, our family started running out of money. No one worked in the household so we only had welfare and what was left of my mother's savings. We were scrimping, but it just wasn't enough to pay the monthly mortgage bills. So my mother, who called us from prison, decided we needed to sell our house. I was stunned. I didn't know where we would go.

To save the money we had left, my mother arranged to send us to a children's home in Kentucky. A fellow inmate had recommended it to her. My brother and I would stay in the dorms with the other kids until our house in Queens, New York, was sold. Then my great-grandmother would come and the three of us would live in the guest house behind the main building.

When I heard about this, I was relieved that there would be a decent place for us to live. I hoped we wouldn't have to worry about money anymore and that I wouldn't have so many responsibilities.

My brother and I spent six months in Kentucky while my great-grandmother was still in New York. Most of the kids at the home were nice, and I felt positive that things would get better. Then my great-grandmother called to tell me that she didn't want to live with us anymore and instead wanted to return to Taiwan. When I heard this, my heart sank. Once more, I felt abandoned.

I returned to New York to discover that my great-grandmother had sold the house to my aunt. My great-grandmother decided to stay a while longer, and we ended up renting the basement from my aunt.

I wasn't crazy about living with my great-grandmother again. I felt as if she'd betrayed me, promising that she would come to Kentucky and then deciding not to. But I was glad that she was staying because I had lived with her for years and at least she was familiar.

The arrangements in the basement were a little different, though. I didn't have a bedroom. I slept on two thick blankets on top of a countertop in the bathroom. It wasn't as bad as it sounds. The bathroom was pretty big and I enjoyed sleeping in it because I had my own corner and my own little window. It made me feel better to be able to look out a window at night looking up at the stars until I fell asleep, wishing my mother were there with me.

> Getting good grades didn't change my loneliness or my worrying about my family.

I got back to New York in time to start eighth grade. But once again, I started feeling too tired to get out of bed for school. I was tired of how my life was, tired of how futile my fight to cope felt. I did well in school, but all I felt was, "So what?" Getting good grades didn't change my loneliness or my worrying about my family. I was so distressed that I started just staying in my "bed" all day, looking out the window, feeling hopeless about my horrid life.

I was embarrassed about things like my mother's incarceration, so I always made up stories if people asked where she was. But every time I told a lie, I got sad; hiding things about myself kept me down.

Then we got kicked out of the basement. One of the neighbors had reported us to the fire department, which considers living in a basement a fire hazard. Now we had to find a new place to live. We got the most decent cheap apartment we could find. My grandmother, who came from Taiwan to help us move, persuaded my great-grandmother (her mother) to continue living with me in the new apartment. Though she was starting to annoy me, there wasn't anyone else able or willing to take her place. None of my aunts and uncles offered to help, which made me feel unwanted and unworthy of being cared for.

Though I tried hard, I barely made it through junior high. But I got into a pretty good high school, and figured I could start anew. I was much more social than before. I seemed to be a cute, funny, sweet boy without a care in the world. Everyone seemed to like me, but I felt that it was just a fake me that didn't represent my true feelings. I acted silly and carefree in public, hoping it would rub off on my true self. The truth was I was still hurting inside, where all the drama was going on.

I had also just realized that I was gay. (Looking back on my childhood, I don't know why I hadn't figured it out earlier; I was always the little diva.) Almost as soon as I recognized my sexuality, I started "coming out" to anyone who asked. I would purposely give little hints like saying that a guy was cute. That would make people ask if I was gay and I would tell them. Most people reacted well; I guess it was never a big surprise to them.

I realized that keeping things in kept me depressed. I was embarrassed about things like my mother's incarceration, so I always made up stories if people asked where she was. But every time I told a lie, I got sad; hiding things about myself kept me down. So I decided I had nothing to hide and to be proud of myself.

My new open attitude didn't help as much as I had hoped. I still didn't find the friends I needed, because even though people said they didn't care that I was gay, I felt like no one was totally comfortable with my sexuality. I started feeling lonely again.

I got careless about my schoolwork, almost as if I had to prove to myself that I wasn't good enough. I felt really tired when the time came every day to get up and go to school, so I just didn't go. I would make up excuses to myself, like "Oh, you woke up late, so don't go to school and just say the next day that you were sick," or "I think

I'm getting sick," when I had a runny nose. My grades went dooowwwnnnn.

I felt like a failure with my family, too. When I came back from Kentucky, I had tried to remake them to match an ideal image. It was an uphill battle.

My family is not known for its togetherness. My mom, uncles, and aunts despise each other, never helping one another out when times get tough. They also have nasty habits. They throw trash on the ground and the men chain-smoke. It also annoyed me that they didn't even try to learn English when they were in an English-speaking country.

I tried creating togetherness by calling my relatives more often. I tried to get my family to eat healthier and act more "sophisticated." I would buy all the groceries and clean the house from top to bottom. I hoped these improvements would counter our poverty. I even watched *My Fair Lady* (a movie about a poor flower girl who is taught to be "proper" by talking, walking, and acting high class) to figure out how to get my family to change. But it was totally hopeless.

You can't change other people; people change only when they want to. It dawned on me that maybe I was ready to change myself.

I had tried to improve my family, but I should've known they were beyond my control. You can't change other people; people change only when they want to. It dawned on me that maybe I was ready to change myself. I knew that I was having trouble again and I decided that I should see a counselor. I was skeptical—if I couldn't find out what was wrong by myself, how could this person do it?—but I went to my school's counselor.

I told the counselor some of the reasons I was depressed: loneliness, my family problems, and my sexuality. He suggested that I try joining a peer group for gay teens. When I showed up at the community center for a group meeting I was somewhat nervous, looking around for people who I might be able to talk to afterward. I wanted to be accepted by the masses and along the way find myself a soul mate. I was grasping the reality of my sexuality and was excited to see how life was for other gay people.

At the center, I met lots of people who I like and now hang with, including my best friend, Effy. Sometimes I feel as though my friends are more family than my real family. They made me feel more comfortable and gave me the courage to be loud. Before when I acted carefree and silly, I was overcompensating, trying to cover up how shy I felt. But now when I'm more outgoing and silly, it feels like the real me.

The feeling of some reassurance gave me hope. I was able to look into myself, and think more clearly about my feelings and what I wanted. I knew I wanted to be "someone" and go to college.

I still had some problems. Because I had missed so much school, I had gotten left back. But I wanted to move forward with my life, not backward. So I dropped out of high school and took the GED and SATs.

I didn't do very well on the SATs. I hadn't studied because I was underestimating my abilities and didn't bother to try. But I didn't want to get down on myself again. I told myself, "You didn't do that great, but it's okay; now you just have to do really great in college for a chance at your dreams." I applied to colleges I thought I could get into, and with a little struggle I got accepted to Brooklyn College.

With the help and encouragement of my friends, I am slowly and successfully getting over my depression.

With the help and encouragement of my friends, I am slowly and successfully getting over my depression. I'm concentrating on what I need to do, like school, and I'm learning to ignore the little things that irritate me. I'm also writing in my journal every day, so there is always a way to let out my feelings. Though I no longer feel the need for the peer group, I still drop by the center once in a while to say hi.

My grandmother moved in with me last year so my great-grandmother could move back to Taiwan, which was fine with me. My mother is set to get out of prison next year, but I don't plan on living with her. I don't feel that connected to her at this point. I missed her a lot when I was younger, but now I feel like I've grown up and it just doesn't matter as much.

I've realized that I have always compared myself to others, and set ridiculous goals. And it would make me depressed if I couldn't reach my goal within a certain time frame. But now I know better. "Baby steps, baby steps" is what I tell myself. I've learned that the best way to deal with my problems is to take small, positive steps toward my goals.

CHANTING HELPS HELPS ME CLEAR MY MIND

by Anonymous

A mumbling sound soars through my head as I try to put my eyes to rest. The noise is like a buzzing that won't let me be!

I listen closely to where the mumbling is coming from . . . my aunts' room. So I creep over to see what they're up to. I push open the door very gently. There I see my two aunts, Kacy and Mary, on their knees, chanting and focusing on a weird object with a scroll inside. They look like they're meditating.

I'm too confused to even ask what's going on. Besides, they'll probably tell me, "You're too young to understand," like they always say when I ask them questions. When I was little I would ask tons of questions about things I heard outside or on television:

"What do they mean when they say the birds and the bees?"

"What's masturbating?"

"Where do babies come from?"

Each question led to the same answer: "You're too young to understand."

So when I saw them chanting and mumbling strange words to a weird object, I said to myself, "Forget this, I'm going to bed with earplugs in my ears and a pillow over my head." Still, I didn't forget all the questions they said I was too young to ask, and I didn't forget their chanting, either.

Six years later, when I was 11, I was going through a really rough time in my life. Because my father had sexually abused me, I was put in foster care with my grandmother. It was a relief, but a whole new beginning for me.

Being in a new home and separated from my mom made me nervous. I still had haunting memories of my father creeping into my room. And dealing with acne and a new school led to nothing but tears in my bed almost every night.

No one wants to wake up in the morning with a whole bunch of stress on their hands.

All this and more made me the girl who sat in a corner covering her face, quiet in front of strangers, but loud as hell around family (while holding every private thought for my diary). People would tell me, "You're too young to walk with your head down," but it was rough becoming a teen, and those dreadful experiences weren't helping me at all.

I was reaching for something to hold on to, that down-on-your-luck searching for something called faith. (Sound familiar?) I wanted to be happy. No one wants to wake up in the morning with a whole bunch of stress on their hands.

Then one day, my aunt Kacy invited me to a women's division meeting at the center where she practices Buddhism. When I saw the weird object with the scroll, I began to remember the suspicious thing my aunts were doing in their room when I was little. Finally, my aunt explained her belief in Buddhism and why she chants.

The way my aunt explained Buddhism made sense to me. She told me that Buddhism isn't about believing in any gods. Instead, it follows the philosophy of a man who, a long time ago, created a method of living in the world that helped him find his true happiness. Part of his method involved chanting or meditating to find peace. Buddhism spread throughout the world because many people accepted his method and felt that meditating cleared their minds.

When Buddhists chant, they say, "Nam-myoho-renge-kyo." "Nam" means devotion. "Myoho" means that reality is only the world as you see it. "Renge" means lotus flower, which grows seeds and blossoms at the same time. This represents cause and effect, showing us how our words and actions have consequences. "Kyo" is sound or teaching.

My aunt said you're supposed to chant twice a day, morning and evening, and to sit up straight and keep your head up. While you're chanting, you must really concentrate on the goals you want to achieve and, most of all, what steps you plan on taking toward these goals. By itself, chanting can't help you achieve happiness. It only helps build your ability to focus on the positive.

My aunt told me that while she chants she focuses on the goals she wants to achieve in her life and on appreciating all that she has achieved so far.

I never learned much more than that about Buddhism, but I started chanting. I focus on what I appreciate in life. Almost every morning I get up and say something like, "Thank you for this glorious day." I figure that complaining about my problems isn't going to solve anything. So when things get to me or when negativity is thrown at me, I stop, chant a few times to clear my head, and let the issue go.

> Chanting isn't magic, but it helps me keep my mind focused on the good things I do have.

Chanting is like meditation—it's something to concentrate on besides what's happening around you. My mind feels more at ease when I chant. It helps me think positively and block most of the negativity out of my head.

I felt low about myself when I started. But as the days went on I began to see a change. Chanting every day, I would think positive things about myself.

Thinking about the positive things about myself and my life makes me feel like I can accomplish almost anything. Chanting isn't magic, but it helps me keep my mind focused on the good things I do have.

WORRIED SICK

by Megan Cohen

I think too much. Not just about really troubling things, but about everything. It takes me 10 to 15 minutes to figure out what to order off a menu, for example. There've been times when I've been up late doing a project and I can't get to sleep because I'm so worried about how I'll feel when the alarm clock wakes me up. I always thought it was a little weird, but I didn't realize how bad my problem was until last year in 10th grade.

That year I had two good friends at school—one from ninth grade and a new girl who'd just transferred there in 10th. As I started to get close to the new girl, I became obsessively worried that she'd become closer with my other friend than she was with me, and then they'd exclude me. I was afraid I'd lose two of the people I cared most about.

Sure enough, they did start to bond, probably because they were annoyed at my constant worrying about the issue. Soon they began to hang out without telling me. Our school lunches became filled with awkward silences in which I felt completely isolated. These silences grew into crushing moments that another friend called "silences of death."

My paranoia didn't stop there. Since I was always thinking about them being such good friends, I began to devalue my other friendships. Sure, my other friend-ships were fun, but how deep were they? Had we ever cried together? Really delved into our histories? I began to create a mental checklist. Nobody passed.

In the end I was left with the one thing I'd been most afraid of: losing two friends. That's when I realized that my overthinking was dragging me down. I wanted to know what I could do about my problem. My editor* suggested I talk to an expert, so I called Jayme Albin, a cognitive-behavioral therapist.

I found out that cognitive-behavioral therapy (CBT) is a type of counseling that focuses on how our thinking influences how we feel and what we do. We all have immediate thoughts when we react to a situation, and these thoughts are based on how we see the world—our "core belief system." The way we see things is based mainly on genetics and our past experiences, including how we were raised.

> I realized that my overthinking was dragging me down. I wanted to know what I could do about my problem.

For example, let's say you get a 75 on a test. A reasonable reaction might be, "I didn't study hard enough for this test, but if I study harder for the next one I'll do better." But if you've grown up believing, "If things aren't 100 percent perfect, I'm a failure," your immediate thought when you look at your grade might be, "I'm an idiot and I'll never get into college." That can cause anxiety.

---

*This essay originally appeared in *New Youth Connections* (Sept./Oct. 2005), so *editor* is referring to Megan's editor at the magazine.

Albin explained that my overthinking is actually a form of anxiety. Anxiety can be useful in small amounts. "It helps us focus, study harder, and so on. It does serve a purpose," Albin said. "It becomes a problem when it starts interfering with everyday life."

But you can't magically get rid of the core beliefs that cause anxiety. "You can't just say, 'Don't be anxious.' That's not helpful," said Albin. It's hard to change your core belief system because it's so deeply ingrained in you, but you can change the way you think.

That's where CBT comes in, according to Albin. "Cognitive behavioral therapy challenges the automatic thoughts in a given situation," she said. The therapist helps you rethink the situation so that you have a more reasonable reaction to it.

It's hard to change your core belief system because it's so deeply ingrained in you, but you can change the way you think.

So when you're feeling anxious, you can learn to think your way out of it by telling yourself that the thoughts causing your anxiety are irrational. Then you try to rethink the situation in a more rational way, until eventually that way of thinking starts coming naturally.

CBT usually lasts about 12 to 18 weeks. By the time you leave therapy you should be so used to thinking yourself through tricky situations that you can sort of act as your own therapist. So, though I'd only met with

Albin once and not for the usual 12 weeks, I decided to try just that.

Albin suggested I start by keeping a thought diary for a few weeks. I was supposed to write down every time I was overthinking or feeling anxious. Then I had to identify and write down the immediate thought that had made me feel that way. If I was worried about my friends being close, maybe my initial thought had been, "They're going to exclude me today." I also had to come up with alternative thoughts to the irrational ones I usually have when I overthink.

If I were in therapy, my therapist and I would then sit down and look at my behavioral pattern. "We'd look to uncover what your tendencies are, like being a perfectionist," said Albin.

Once we saw how I reacted in certain situations, we would talk about how I could've reacted differently. I'd be able to start changing my thoughts and, eventually, my behavior.

For three weeks I wrote in the diary every time I found myself thinking about something too long. In my first entry I wrote, "Today I couldn't even decide what I wanted for lunch, let alone who to eat it with. An everything bagel with butter or a plain bagel with tuna? Or maybe pizza?"

I was frustrated with my indecisiveness, but I didn't use the reasoning process Albin had suggested. It seemed stupid for something as small as picking out lunch. I figured it would take more energy to chart out my thoughts than to just make a decision.

But writing down my thoughts over the three weeks made me realize how often I can't make the most trivial decisions, like whether to turn right or left on a street corner. I started to realize how much energy indecision takes from me. I also started to realize why I overthink sometimes.

> **Writing down my thoughts over three weeks made me realize how often I can't make the most trivial decisions. I started to realize how much energy indecision takes from me.**

One night about a week into my diary experiment, I "yelled" at a friend online, telling him he ignored me and thought he was superior to me. Even as I was accusing him, I didn't know why I was doing it.

I finally asked myself what I was doing, and realized that I was stressed and worried about another friend of mine. My anger had nothing to do with the person I'd yelled at. I told him to forget about everything I'd said, that I hadn't meant to take it out on him. I wrote in my diary that night, "This feels like a crucial point of progress and something I definitely would've overlooked before."

Now I can tell when I'm about to obsess over a situation, and I'm starting to understand why I do it. When I'm upset, I try to block out what's really upsetting me by upsetting myself over something less important.

And I'm still not sure why I overthink decisions like what I want to eat for lunch. Maybe I'm afraid of making the wrong choice and having nobody to blame for it but myself, even if it's just lunch. Now I realize that I just need to let it go and decide.

A couple of weeks ago, my notoriously anxious middle-aged cousin came to visit my family. It's hard to spend time with her because she's always worrying that things that are going just fine will fall apart, like she'll suddenly lose her job one day. She creates an unbearable uneasiness around her. She gave me a glimpse into what I could become if I don't stop this now.

I think I'm getting better already. At least I've decided one thing: I don't like that I overthink. It took me a really long time to figure that out, but I've finally gotten here. Now I just need to notice when I'm doing it, and then rethink the situation more rationally. This is one decision I'll be sure to stick to.

MY FAVORITE ESCAPE

by Martin Smith

As a little boy I always dreamed of becoming an NBA basketball player. When I was about 5 or 6 years old, I began to watch it on television and I'd always root for my favorite team, the New York Knicks.

While I was in elementary school, I'd play ball during recess and I'd always manage to score more points than my classmates. At a young age, I realized I was good at this sport. We played in gym class a lot. I played position guard or sometimes forward, since I was one of the tallest people on the team.

One day we were playing in gym and the other team took the lead 58 to 57 with 10 seconds left. My nervous coach called a time-out and decided that I would take the last shot.

My heart was beating out of my chest as I passed the ball to my closest team member and ran to the three-point line. I got the ball back, and with two seconds left I closed my eyes and took the best shot I could.

I didn't even see if the shot went in or not, but when I opened my eyes, the scoreboard read 60 to 58! Everybody came rushing toward me. I had won the game for the team! It was the first time in my life that I had a dream that came true.

Ever since that day, basketball has played a big role in my life. Basketball gives me a chance

Basketball gives me a chance to escape from my problems and helps me feel good about myself.

to escape from my problems and helps me feel good about myself.

When I got a little older, my big brother taught me how to play according to street ball rules. The rules in street ball are different from rules in an official game because there are more tricks you can get away with. We played in the park around the corner where everybody from the neighborhood went to play.

The first time I went there to play, all the kids were looking at me because they didn't know me. I didn't really feel comfortable. Most of the guys were older, taller, and bigger than me, so they took advantage of the court. They would run full-court basketball games so that nobody else could play.

I was there with my brother and a couple of our friends from the neighborhood. We told the guys on the court that we wanted to play, but they said no. Maybe they thought we couldn't play because we were small and young. So we challenged them to a 10-point game.

I never thought that we'd be able to compete with the older guys, but we won the game 10 to 9.

We were all so happy that we were screaming and jumping with excitement. At that moment I was in heaven—couldn't nobody tell me nothing. And after a while, the older kids started going to the court a few blocks down.

After that day I had a better understanding of how to play the game. My brother and I would play every day in the summertime trying to get better and better. I began to look at basketball as more than just a sport. My goal was to become a pro player and I was on a mission to make my dream come true. That kept me motivated to move forward every day.

Basketball also helped me with the problems I was facing in my everyday life. When I got stressed about everything going on at home between me and my brother and my godfather, I'd play ball to calm down.

It was like every time I played basketball, all my pain, stress, and worries just went away. When I was on the court I wouldn't think about the chores that I had to do when I got home, or my godfather screaming at me because I forgot to clean my room.

Every time I played I got a sense of freedom, and basketball became my favorite escape. Every time I won I felt good about myself and relieved. I didn't like to lose while playing basketball, because that sense of freedom would disappear. I'd get frustrated and ask for a rematch until I won.

> **Every time I played I got a sense of freedom, and basketball became my favorite escape.**

When I was old enough, I joined a junior Knicks basketball team. At the time, I was going through a lot of family problems. My godfather was very strict with me. I was having problems keeping up with the work in school, and I felt pressured to pass all my classes and get good grades. Basketball got me out of the house so I didn't have to deal with my godfather.

In the past I'd always dealt with my stress by smoking weed. But the coach would give random drug tests. If one came up positive you were off the team, just like that, no second chances. I loved the game so much I couldn't do anything to risk getting kicked off. Now, when I got upset, I couldn't just go and smoke. I had to deal with my stress in a different way, which was to go and play basketball.

Being on the team was a very good experience for me. I met new people who shared dreams like mine. It was easier for me to relate to them because we went through similar situations at home, like not having enough food in the house and always getting into trouble at home and school. The other kids on the team were cool and really friendly, and we were very close.

I'm too old for the junior Knicks now, but basketball still plays a major role in my life. These days I play for my high school. Being on the team puts me in the public eye, has helped me meet girls, and has made me one of the popular kids at school. And once again, I get the chance to do something that really makes me feel good about myself.

NEVER GOOD ENOUGH

by Chimore T. Mack

Some people think I am a working machine. I like working because I don't like staying in the house and I don't like to be broke. I'd rather put in a day's work than sit up in the house doing nothing. But sometimes, I get obsessed with work.

My life experiences make me crave stability and independence, and I see hard work as the way to achieve those things. My grandmother devoted her life to raising my siblings and me. I felt good that she gave me stability, but I often felt sad that my grandmother had to work so hard. I sometimes felt like I was a burden and was eager to work so I could carry my own weight.

I'd heard plenty of stories about kids who aged out of foster care and ended up homeless. I was determined not to let it happen to me.

My grandmother taught me at a very young age that hard work pays off. I believe that, because it's proven true for me as I've gone through the difficult process of aging out* and learning to survive without the foster care agency backing me up.

A lot of people try to scare you about aging out: "Oh, you're going to end up in a shelter and no one is going to be there." That's enough to make some people want to give up before they even try to make it on their own.

---

*Aging out refers to when a person in foster care turns 21 and he or she leaves the foster care system and transitions to independent living.

However, it made me want to fight and prove to people that I could do it.

KEEPING A ROOF OVER MY HEAD

The first obstacle was finding a job. In the year before I turned 21, I applied to numerous jobs. Many of them never called me back. I worried and sometimes felt down on myself, but I never gave up because my grandmother always told me to keep trying. Just like singer Aaliyah said, "Dust yourself off and try again." I also prayed, and eventually I got a job working at a chain retail clothing store.

Last Christmas, right after turning 21, I was working at the clothing store and giving my foster mother rent money every two weeks so I could continue to live there. I didn't have anywhere else to stay at that point because the subsidized housing my agency was working on getting me wasn't ready.

It felt great to be working, but after the holidays, the store started cutting my hours. I had to tap into my savings to pay the rent, which meant I couldn't save for the things I'd need when I got my own place. That's when I learned that retail jobs weren't very stable. I decided that I needed a second job.

Finally, things started falling into place. My housing came through in early spring, and I ended up getting another job so that I could handle living on my own. I worked at the store in the mornings and afternoons, wrote for *Represent* (a magazine written by and for teens in foster care) two days a week, and worked at a fast-food restaurant four nights per week.

When I started working at the restaurant I was glad to get another job, although my sister was concerned I might burn out. "Make sure you don't bite what you can't chew," she warned.

> **Getting paid every two weeks and being able to buy the things I wanted and needed felt great. The downside was stress and not getting enough sleep.**

But I knew that responsibilities had to be taken care of. I had to make sure rent and bills were paid, the fridge was full, and clothes were on my back. I'd heard plenty of stories about kids who aged out of foster care and ended up homeless. I was determined not to let it happen to me.

OBSESSED WITH WORK

I often struggled to find the right balance between work and time for myself. I had a list of practical goals: building up my credit, staying afloat with the rent and bills, saving some money. Getting paid every two weeks and being able to buy the things I wanted and needed felt great.

The downside was stress and not getting enough sleep. Sometimes I wouldn't get home from the restaurant until four or five in the morning and would only get an hour or two of sleep before I had to get ready for my shift at

the store. That messed up my job performance and sometimes made me late, which caused me more stress.

But my biggest problem was that sometimes I
couldn't stop thinking about work, especially if my boss
told me that I didn't do what I was supposed to. When
I felt that the job wasn't done right, I stressed myself
afterward by thinking, "Man, why didn't I do that?" I
couldn't relax, even when I wasn't at work. I doubted
myself, and I felt like I had to work harder and be better.
I couldn't let it go.

I think this goes back to me being a perfectionist. I'd
always beat myself up when I'd get a low grade because
my grandmother wanted to see only good grades on my
report card. She was very strict because she always strived
for the best and she wanted me to have the best, too.

I guess I carried that feeling into foster care. But unlike
my grandmother, the people around me after I went into
care weren't as supportive. My foster mother and even
friends were very critical. They'd throw my mistakes in
my face and they never praised me. It really hurt, and I
would try, once again, to do better. But it seemed like it
was never good enough.

Although I knew my foster mother was trying to push
me, she made me feel bad about myself. I didn't need
that. It was different from my grandmother pushing me;
she only wanted me to succeed and make my dreams
become reality, and that was more positive and uplifting.

One thing that helps me deal with negativity—whether it's coming from me or someone else—is to think about how far I've come in achieving my goals. Work has given me a sense of purpose and helped me realize the person I want to be: someone with confidence who can do a job well, but who also has dreams and goals bigger than the work at hand.

WORK-LIFE BALANCE

But I would like a better balance between my work and the rest of my life. I want to go out and chill with my family and friends, and I don't want work to mess up my health. It's hard for me to settle down and forget about work, though. My friends are like, "Damn, you always talking about work and bills."

Wanting to be perfect kept me from seeing that anyone would struggle with the kinds of hours I was working between my two jobs. I was also blinded by the validation of getting two paychecks.

> **Wanting to be perfect kept me from seeing that anyone would struggle with the kinds of hours I was working between my two jobs.**

But then the restaurant started cutting my hours without warning. I'd get to work and they'd tell me they didn't need me to come in after all. I thought about how hard I'd been working to do my job well. They didn't seem to appreciate it at all, so I decided to quit.

Soon after, I got fired from the store. I'd been late a lot, but I was also fired for something I thought would please my boss. We were supposed to try to get customers to apply for a store credit card, and if they were accepted, they got a discount and we were rewarded with employee points.

What I didn't understand was that we were only supposed to give discounts to customers who were approved for the credit card—I'd been giving discounts to customers just for applying. I was making the customers happy; I didn't know I wasn't supposed to give those discounts until I got a call from the store's investigator telling me I'd caused the store to come up short.

A BLESSING IN DISGUISE

At first, it seemed like this was a disaster. But not having those two jobs turned out to be kind of a blessing. It freed me up to apply for jobs that fit better with my long-term goals.

I recently got a new job working as a receptionist at a tax preparation company. I love it because I get plenty of hours and experience working in an office. My supervisor is supportive, and that makes me feel like I am capable of doing the job. I feel accepted for who I am, and that makes me feel more free.

I also checked out a program that would train me for a good office job and give me college credit. The application process took a month: I had to take some skills tests and attend several trainings. Though I recently found out I wasn't accepted to the program for this semester, I'm not beating myself up about it this time. I felt good that I'd taken a chance, and I learned a lot. They encouraged me to apply for next semester, and I'm going to try again.

One thing that helps me deal with negativity—whether it's coming from me or someone else—is to think about how far I've come in achieving my goals.

Now, I want to work on enjoying the simple things in life—making time for friends and family, walking my dog, going to museums, and learning how to cook. Lately I have been spending time discovering my spirituality. And I love that I sometimes just stay home to relax, watch a movie, and have fun with my dog. It reminds me that life is not always about responsibilities. I have to learn to make time to enjoy it without worrying about the risks so much.

FEELING THE PRESSURE

by Jennifer Baum

It's really late and you're supposed to be home. You've tried to call your house, but you can't get through. You try to hail a cab, but for some reason none will stop for you. It's getting later and later, and you know that you're going to be in trouble once you get home. Finally, a cab slows down. You breathe a sigh of relief and think you'll be home in no time. But the driver takes one look at you and keeps on going.

This is what happened to a friend of Shantonu, 18. In the end, he got so angry and stressed out that he ran to the corner, picked up a garbage can, and threw it through the cab's window.

We've all been stressed out at one time or another. It can last for weeks or months and can result from many things. School can be stressful. Miles, 15, said he feels a lot of pressure when there's a big report due. He said that he often waits until the last minute to get it done. "I usually cut corners and don't do the report as well as I could," he explained. "Then I feel frustrated with myself for not getting it done better."

You also might be pressured by your parents or friends to do things. My parents and I get into fights about my schoolwork. They always seem to be on my back about something. They don't realize that sometimes I like to be left alone.

Dr. Richard Dudley, a psychiatrist who works with teens, said, "Sometimes parents don't realize that teenagers need their own space, or that they're becoming their own person and don't need to depend on Mommy and Daddy so much anymore."

Everyday things, like taking care of a little brother or sister or other relative can be stressful, too. Danny, 17, lives with his 90-year-old grandmother and has to take care of her. "It's kind of a burden," he said. "There's lots of pressure on my parents and me."

Sometimes stress comes from inside—teens are unhappy with themselves, the way they look, or the need to fit in.

And stress changes us. When people feel stressed out, sometimes their bodies react in unhealthy ways. "I might lose sleep," said Danny. "Sometimes I get headaches or pains, and I really don't know what it's from. And my doctor said pimples can be caused by stress."

Shantonu also complained of headaches and trouble sleeping. Dr. Dudley said changes in sleeping patterns are very common. A lot of "normal body stuff" gets messed up, too: people might get nervous, shake or sweat, lose their appetite, or feel hungry. People get stomachaches and back pain, and some can even develop ulcers. A woman's menstrual cycle can also get messed up, and the immune system doesn't work well

"Being stressed out preoccupies you," said Dr. Dudley. You're less able to think things through, less able to concentrate or remember things.

99

when you are under a lot of stress. When you're stressed, you're also more susceptible to getting colds.

Psychological symptoms can occur as well. "Being stressed out preoccupies you," said Dr. Dudley. You're less able to think things through, less able to concentrate or remember things.

When these things start happening, many teens try to ignore the real reasons or block them out. Drugs, alcohol, or sex are a few of the ways they hide their problems.

"If I'm very upset about something, I might drink," said Danny. But he tries not to drink very often, and he warned that drinking or doing drugs is not a good solution to stress. "You just cushion the problem for a minute when you do those things," he said. "But you're still going to have the same problem after."

Dr. Dudley said that a lot of teens also use sex to cover up their problems. "Say your boyfriend left you," he explained. "Instead of thinking rationally, you run around with 15 different guys being very promiscuous." Dr. Dudley cautioned that this strategy never works. He said the problem "won't go away by itself."

There are many positive ways to help reduce stress. "I try to stop what I'm doing," explained Miles. "Then I calm down, watch sports on TV, and then go back to what I'm doing." Shantonu said that he meditates to relieve the pressure, and that swimming also helps. Dr.

Dudley said that eating right, taking time to relax, and getting enough sleep and exercise can be really helpful.

Shantonu agrees: "Take deep breaths, relax, and stay away from drugs and alcohol, and stressful activities." For Danny, "Talking to a friend is a big outlet."

Dr. Dudley agrees: "It's hard to work it out by yourself." If you are feeling stressed out, you should talk to someone you feel close to, such as friends, a doctor, or a teacher. Sometimes it's hard to find a psychiatrist or counselor to talk to, but schools and youth centers can tell you where to find help. "People I know have seen therapists or are in peer groups that help them," added Danny.

Sometimes it's hard to find a psychiatrist or counselor to talk to, but schools and youth centers can tell you where to find help.

Stress is not the end of the world. "Stress isn't always bad," said Dr. Dudley. "Falling in love can be stressful." We always get uptight about changing and adjusting to new relationships and new situations.

If you are feeling stressed, there are always people to talk to, people who are willing to help. You just have to be willing to talk to them. It's nothing to be ashamed of.

I LEAVE MY ANGER AT THE RINK

by David A. Rodriguez

*P*laying baseball in my community's league as a little kid, I was an excellent hitter but a horrible fielder. I wanted to play something that I could be really good at, so I could feel good about myself as an athlete.

So I started playing ice hockey in fourth grade at a local skating rink. My older brother had played in their house league. I loved the sport, but I felt out of place there. Not many of the players spoke to me. Maybe it was because most of them knew each other already. Or maybe it was because I was Hispanic and they were all white, or because I was smaller than most of them.

> **Feeling like the outsider added emotion to my game, and the game also helped me release my anger. Pushing my body to its limits is the best way to get out my stress.**

Whatever the reason, I felt a prejudice that led them to underestimate or ignore my skills. I almost scored from behind the net once or twice—how much skill did I need to show to be accepted?

I felt that I had to prove myself in every game, whether it meant just playing hard defense or scoring two goals. I did everything I could to win their respect.

Feeling like the outsider added emotion to my game, and the game also helped me release my anger. Pushing my body to its limits is the best way to get out my stress.

I was having a tough time in school, too. I was picked on a lot by the other students, mostly because I was smaller (though not anymore), and I got into a lot of fights.

On top of that, my punishments at school were sometimes harsher than those of the kid attacking me, so I was angry at being treated unfairly in general. Playing ice hockey was my way of getting out my anger and having something to be proud of when life sucked.

> I was picked on a lot by the other students, mostly because I was smaller (though not anymore), and I got into a lot of fights.

My first hockey goal came to me in my second season in the ice hockey league. We were tied 2–2 and I pushed myself over the blue line, already tired and sweating from a long shift. My teammate fired the puck at the goalie: My heart pounded and jumped in my throat as I saw the rebound ricochet out in front of me.

Bending my arms back, and with one swift flick of my wrists, I shot the puck into the net. Goal!

I threw my arms in the air as I skated to a halt, to be greeted by my other teammates. "Sweet goal," one of them said. It made me feel that all the practice had finally paid off.

My relationship with the players didn't change much, though. They'd been playing longer than I had and were stuck up about their skills. Most of the time during games, they only passed the puck to their friends. Sometimes I felt like I was playing alone. I was able to play and improve my skills, but there was no real teamwork.

I played ice hockey for five years. It was fun and I had some interesting moments, from a few breakaway goals to almost scoring from behind the net.

But this past spring I played in a roller hockey league and liked that a lot better. (Ice hockey is played with ice skates on ice and is much faster than roller hockey, which is played with roller skates on pavement.) There is a lot more teamwork, and the players have more diverse backgrounds, including Hispanic, Italian, and Asian.

When I play now, I still have some of the same feelings when I played ice hockey. I still carry a lot of anger with me, but I'm not a hot-headed, aggressive person. I keep all of my anger on the pavement. When I play roller hockey I get out all of my anger and stress, and generally feel better afterward.

STRESS IS NOT JUST FOR SENIORS

by Tanya Owens

Most people think that senior year is the most stressful time of high school. Ha! I'm a junior and I knew school would be a lot of work, but I didn't expect it to be so much that I would lose my mind. I thought I could handle it without any problems, but I was wrong.

Three weeks after school started I became really mad and aggravated because I didn't think I could do it all. My school makes us do nine portfolios, which are big projects consisting of work done from ninth grade to the current school year.

One day I came home from school and went in my room to do my work, and I started jumping from one project to the next.

I came home from school and went in my room to do my work, and I started jumping from one project to the next. I had so much to do I couldn't concentrate on one thing.

I had so much to do I couldn't concentrate on one thing.

First, I was working on the four parts of my autobiography portfolio. I had to write my life story, prepare a résumé, write out my career and college plans, and attach them nicely to three letters of recommendation (which, fortunately, I did have already).

I wanted to finish all the parts before winter vacation so my teacher could read them over. That way I would get a chance to revise them before handing in the final versions for a grade. But all the parts had to be typed, and I could never find the time to type at school because other kids in my class were always on the computers.

And I don't have a computer at home. I started to worry that I wouldn't finish on time.

Thinking about my college plans for my autobiography portfolio made me remember that I was going to take the PSAT in a few weeks. My teachers had been talking about the test since the first week of school. I was scared I wasn't going to do well, and therefore I wouldn't be prepared to take the SAT in May.

I especially feared the math section because: (1) I hate the subject, (2) I hadn't learned a lot of the hard math that is on the test, and (3) I really didn't know what the test was like. I bought an SAT practice book, but every time I took the quizzes in the book my answers were wrong and I still didn't understand what I was doing. At my school I was taking PSAT classes on Fridays, but they didn't start until three weeks before the test. I felt it wasn't enough time to learn all I'd need to know.

I felt like my head was about to explode. So I decided to call my 25-year-old sister, Tina. She has a job where she has to be organized and she always gives me good advice. She's always been there when I needed someone to talk to. In school she had to work hard to keep her grades up, so I felt she would have some insight into what I was going through.

"Hi, Tina, can I talk to you?" I said.

"Hi, Tan, sure," she said. "What's up?"

"I'm so stressed I can't take it," I told her. "I bought an SAT book but I feel I'm gonna fail. And besides that, I can't do my portfolio."

"Take one thing at a time, don't stress yourself so much," Tina said. "The PSAT is just practice to see what you need to learn and it doesn't count as far as the colleges are concerned. They just look at your real SAT score. Just study as much as you can."

"Yeah, but my portfolio is bugging me. I'm working on my autobiography, but I haven't started typing yet and I have two other parts of it to do also," I said, complaining away. "And do you know that I'll still have other portfolios left to do?"

"When are all these due?" she said.

"Just the autobiography and its parts are due in January," I said. "The other portfolios are either due at the end of the school year or they'll be done during senior year."

"Well, stick to the autobiography," Tina told me. "Don't worry about the others that are due later until you finish that one. You'll be okay."

"Okay, thanks Tin," I said.

Talking to my sister made me calm down a little. Hey, I'm too young to get gray hair from being so stressed out. So I decided to try what my sister told me.

I'm too young to get gray hair from being so stressed out.

109

Since that day, I've started making real progress. I took the PSAT in October and wasn't nervous. I finished my autobiography and typed it, too, by finally getting a spot on a computer at school.

I still have a big project to do for each of my classes but I'm not getting stressed out anymore. I just do as much as I can and take one thing at a time. I realize the less time you spend worrying, the more time you have to get stuff done.

NATURE IS MY SALVATION

by Emily Orchier

Have you ever been so depressed that you can't sleep? (Too unhappy.) You also can't eat. (There's never anything good in the house, and even if there were, it would be tasteless.) You can't read. (No attention span.) You have no friends to call up on the phone and nothing good is on TV. So you sigh, press your face down harder into your pillow, lament, and shed a few tears.

The thought of moving was unbearable. I felt as if all of my body parts were weighed down by a ton of bricks. I couldn't remember the last time I had gone outside.

This was my life two years ago. I had just turned 14 and I felt bleak. As I lay in my bed one Saturday, my mother peeked into my room to make her regular "Is Em still alive?" check. Even I knew that if I spent much more time like this, she would have to begin dusting me.

"Hi, hon," my mom said. I grunted in acknowledgment.

"How are you feeling today, sweetheart?" she asked.

"How do you think?" I replied sarcastically.

After suggesting a number of things for me to do (that I promptly rejected), my mother made her move:

"Emily! Get dressed! I'm taking the dog out for a walk, and you are coming with me!"

"Why?" I moaned.

"Because it will make you feel better."

The thought of moving was unbearable. I felt as if all of my body parts were weighed down by a ton of bricks.

I couldn't remember the last time I had gone outside. Somehow I found the strength to slip on a pair of jeans and a black sweatshirt. My mother was waiting at the door for me, leash in hand and dog at her side.

"I still don't get how going for a walk will make me feel any better," I complained.

My mother gave me a look and opened the door. We stepped outside. It was one of those unusually warm March days when you could get away with jeans and a sweatshirt, but the signs of spring had yet to appear. It had been a long time since the warmth of the sun had touched my cheeks.

My mother led the dog and me to the aqueduct, a dirt path that historically carried water underground to a nearby city. Now its sole purpose is for outdoor recreation. I carried on and complained throughout the entire excursion.

"I'm tired! This is boring, Mother. When can we go home?"

"Not just yet," she'd say.

My mother stopped to say hi to every jogger, dog walker, runner, and bicyclist who passed us. Sometimes she would get into a conversation with someone. She exerted herself—made herself happier than I knew she felt from being around me. They would talk about the weather, dogs, and other topics of small talk. I thought it was all so senseless.

After walking for what seemed to be an eternity, my mother finally said that it was time to turn around. She was glowing.

When we got home, I was confronted with a new sensation. It was as if the ton of bricks had been lifted off my heart. But I didn't let this feeling last long, because I didn't know how to handle it. For nearly a year I had been immersed in sadness. How could I learn to feel happy again?

I soon found myself back in my room, in a comfortable funk. But that walk had done something to me. I didn't know how or why, but for a moment in time life almost felt all right. A week went by, and a new Saturday found me asking my mother if we could go for another walk.

April arrived, and with it an array of beautiful spring blossoms. I began to take my dog out for her weekend mid-morning walks. We would go across the street to a big field, which led to small paths lined with daffodils, which in turn led to orchards with apple blossoms.

Walking became an everyday affair for me, and I began to acknowledge the powerful solace that it brought me.

Smaller fields abounded with blooming dogwood and magnolia trees and scattered patches of tiny purple wildflowers. Walking there, I was overcome by beautiful fragrances. It became my little slice of heaven. I was healing.

So it came to pass that I was the official dog walker of the family. Walking became an everyday affair for me, and I began to acknowledge the powerful solace that it brought me.

Late that summer, I remembered a pond that my parents used to take me to when I was a very small child. Halsey Pond was its name. One morning I decided to make the trek over to Halsey.

It was very long for a walk, taking more than two hours to get there and back. But as soon as I laid eyes on the place, I knew that I loved it. Everywhere I looked, there was life—ducks, geese, deer, turkeys, water snakes, turtles, squirrels, and giant carp. I began to wake up early in the morning to take my daily pilgrimage there.

If walking was my spiritual practice, then Halsey was a wonderful sanctuary. I felt such peace and serenity while I was there. I also made many friends at the pond, and greeted every jogger, runner, dog walker, or bicyclist who came my way.

My depression lifted in time. Now that I have been feeling so much better, I also have become much busier and have less time to walk. I no longer walk to Halsey Pond every morning. But I do make sure that I get out every day, if only for a little while. Walking was my salvation from the throes of depression. It is strong medicine for the soul.

THE AMERICAN DREAM GAVE ME ANXIETY ATTACKS

by Abdouramane Barry

As a teen boy in my home country of Guinea, West Africa, I didn't have the same worries as many of my peers. Most parents sent their sons to school just long enough to learn the basics, and then they sent them to work to help their families financially.

But my father was in the United States, where he was earning about three times what he would have made in Guinea. Besides this, my father has only one wife and five kids, while plenty of fathers in Guinea have four wives and more than 20 kids to support. With most of my needs met, the only things I worried about were going to school, eating, flirting with girls, and acting like I was the king.

I knew I would one day join my father in the United States, but I never thought about the responsibility this implied: that I would eventually have to contribute to the support of my family. Nor did I understand how dif-

I believed, as most people did in Guinea, that if you lived in the United States you could afford anything.

ficult my dad's position was. I used to be mad that he didn't send us more money. I believed, as most people did in Guinea, that if you lived in the United States you could afford anything.

When I was 15, my father arranged for me to move to the United States. My friends told me I was blessed, that I'd be rich soon, and that they wished they could follow in my footsteps. They were even more excited than I was.

Like my friends, I thought I would be the happiest person alive once I got to this country. I was ready to have fun and become well known and successful. Yet almost as soon as I arrived, I realized that I was totally mistaken about life here. Gradually I discovered something I hadn't experienced before: anxiety.

DAD'S SACRIFICES

My father is 47. He is diabetic but works long hours, from 6 a.m. to 11 p.m., without resting. He has no choice because he supports all our family and relatives living in Africa, whether in Guinea, Senegal, or Ivory Coast. He is a simple taxi driver who earns just a few dollars a day, yet he has overwhelming financial responsibilities.

When I arrived and saw how hard he worked for us, I felt sad. I never knew that my father was living in a single room here; in my country, my family owns three houses and two cars, all bought with the money my dad sent home. It was precisely because he gave us everything we needed that I thought he must own many properties here, too. I never imagined what my dad was sacrificing to give us the life we enjoyed back home. Literally, he would rather die of hunger than let us starve.

> **I never imagined what my dad was sacrificing to give us the life we enjoyed back home. Literally, he would rather die of hunger than let us starve.**

I also felt sad because most of my family members back home still had the misconceptions I'd had. They called him often, asking him to send money or other things. I wanted to blurt out that they should find themselves jobs and leave my father alone, but I knew my father would be mad at me if I did that because he doesn't want anyone to think badly about us.

DREARY AND UNINSPIRED

I never showed my father my sadness. Instead, I became troubled in my own mind. I now understood that if I didn't study hard and become successful, I would be loaded with his same financial burdens and never enjoy life. I also wished I could help my dad out immediately. The boy who'd never thought of making money now wanted a job right away.

I don't think the stress really kicked in, though, until I heard that one of my friends back in Guinea—who was only a year older than me—had started a successful import and export business. And he planned to expand his entrepreneurial activities by building houses and opening stores in some neighboring countries.

With all of the money he'd made, he'd been able to help his father with family expenses and was even getting ready to send his mom to Mecca. (Mecca is an Islamic holy site in Saudi Arabia that Muslims are supposed to visit if they can, but many are too poor to afford the trip.)

I couldn't feel happy for my homeboy who was working hard to achieve his goals; instead I was jealous and dying to do the same. I started to compare myself with my friends both here and in Guinea. Most of my Guinean friends in New York were full of ideas about how to make money—whether it was to buy a taxi and rent it to a driver while they were in school, or to send money home so business partners there could open stores or other enterprises.

> **I was so busy critiquing myself that I couldn't see opportunities.**

How was everyone else so imaginative and determined, while I was dreary and uninspired? As this question took over my mind, it made me even less likely to think creatively. I was so busy critiquing myself that I couldn't see opportunities. Once my younger cousin in Guinea asked me to collect used, unwanted phones here and send them to him for resale. Instead of getting excited about this business idea, I blamed myself for being less entrepreneurial than even my little cousin.

NO JOB, NO MONEY

I decided that I wouldn't ask my father for anything anymore. I felt bad every time I asked him for money to buy clothes, food, or a movie ticket. My friends had found retail and food service jobs and had their own income. They were all a year or two older than me, which made it easier for them to get hired. But this was no consolation; I felt younger, weaker, and lower than my friends. I would look at them and think, "I can't even buy my own underwear."

I told myself that I had the advantage of living in the United States with papers, something that many people dream of having, and it was time I made the most of it. "I will not let any of my friends get ahead of me," I said to myself angrily.

The school year was almost over, so I decided to look for a job. I went into it with the same pessimistic mindset: I felt useless and always thought of what I didn't have to offer, instead of my advantages. But even if I'd been optimistic, it probably wouldn't have helped. I was 16, and everywhere I went, people told me that I was too young.

My father tried to discourage me from getting a job. He worried I'd stop studying and focus more on earning money. He wants me to get the best education possible so that I don't suffer as he does, working hard for little benefit. Though I wanted the same thing for myself, I ignored his concerns and my own, because I couldn't get past the pressing desire to take care of my own expenses and relieve my father's burden.

As my self-esteem shrank, I started having panic attacks.

ABOUT TO DIE?

The first time I experienced a panic attack, I thought I was about to die. I was in the computer lab after school, doing my history homework. Suddenly I was trembling and cold; my heart was beating so fast that I thought I was having a heart attack. Everything around me looked blurry.

I got up from my chair, so dizzy that I knocked a garbage can over as I left the room. I held on to the wall and walked down the hallway, wishing I could lie on the floor. Feeling weak, I struggled up the stairs to the school nurse's office.

She made me sit there while she called my father, who came and took me to the emergency room. They gave me tests and took two X-rays, and told me that they didn't see anything wrong. I never knew you could be sick without anything being wrong with your body—certainly not as sick as I was feeling. I was afraid I was losing my mind.

We went home, but over the next few weeks the panic attacks kept coming. Some lasted as long as four days. I would get dizzy and short of breath whenever I left my house. I didn't feel like myself at all; I had an almost out-of-body experience, like my mind was somewhere else, dreaming what was happening to me. This strengthened my impression that I was going crazy.

I wanted to stay home forever and never go outside again. I talked to my father about what was happening. He took me to three more doctors, and they all said exactly the same thing: "He is fine," as though they could feel what I was feeling. I wasn't faking sickness, but in one way, they were right: Nothing physically was wrong, except that I expected too much of myself and wanted more than what God gave me. My thoughts were changing my reality.

NOT SO SIMPLE

One of the doctors talked to my father about anxiety and the symptoms it can cause, and suggested that my father try to talk to me. So in the car on the way home from the hospital, my dad asked in a concerned voice, "How are you feeling now?" He looked sad and was driving slowly.

"I don't really know how I am feeling right now," I replied.

"Do you know what you should do?" he asked.

I looked at him, puzzled, wondering what he'd say.

"Listen carefully: I am going to tell you the best medicine you could ever get for these panics," he said. "You should eat well, the way you are supposed to, and not care about what others have that you don't." He looked at me and continued, "You cannot defy your destiny. It is the way God wants it to be, and none of us can do anything about it. Go to school and study as hard as you can. That's the only way you can change your actual life." He took a deep breath. "If this doesn't change things for you, tell me and I will prescribe something else. Okay?"

"Okay," I murmured. I felt confused and tongue-tied. I doubted that curing myself would be as simple as my dad suggested. Every time I tried to concentrate on other things, like school, my head would fill with the same obsessive desire for enough money to buy what I wanted, let my dad retire, send my parents to Mecca, and help my family.

RELAXED AND REAL AGAIN

My guidance counselor knew that I'd gone to the school nurse and that things were not right with me. When I started missing school regularly because of the panics, he questioned me about what was going on, and I told him how I was feeling. He referred me to the school psychologist, who referred me to a psychiatrist (a medical doctor who treats problems of the mind).

The psychiatrist, after talking to me about my panics, prescribed me medication, which I began taking last March. After being on the medication for four or five weeks, I started feeling relaxed and real again. I am still taking the medication and talking to the school psychologist.

When we meet, she always asks how I am feeling. Since I started feeling better, I've usually responded, "I'm good—busy with college stuff." So at this point, we usually spend our time talking about and researching colleges and scholarships. I've found her very helpful; she always gives me something to focus on.

By making me calmer, the medication allows me to appreciate the wisdom of my dad's advice. Even if there are some things other people have that I don't, there are other things I have that they don't. For instance, I'm lucky to have a good father like him; many of my friends don't get along well with

The medication allows me to appreciate the wisdom of my dad's advice. Even if there are some things other people have that I don't, there are other things I have that they don't.

their parents. I also know I am smart and learn fast, I'm good at sports, and I have friends who like me a lot and tell me how nice I am at least once a day. Now I try to better appreciate myself and what I have.

After taking the medication for a while and talking to the psychologist, I've also found that I have a different view of the world I live in. Life is uncertain: You can wake up today with your loved ones by your side as easily as you can wake up tomorrow without them. There are many things we can't control. Even though this sounds bleak, I've found that I feel happier and less desperate when I reflect that I'm not in control of life, because I'm convinced that God rules.

MANAGING WHAT I CAN

Now, I'm glad to say I am more focused on my education than my financial situation. As my father told me, through schooling I can get everything I dream of, and I try to keep that in mind always. My problems haven't disappeared, but I feel much better physically, and better able to manage school and responsibilities.

I sometimes experience symptoms like shortness of breath and dizziness, even when I'm taking medication. But I'm able to calm myself down using my psychologist's advice: I close my eyes, breathe in and out 10 times, and remember that anxiety by itself never killed anyone. Now that I'm used to the physical feeling of panic and know what is happening to me, it's easier to stay cool. But eventually I'd like to get to the point where I can manage my anxiety without medication.

Each day I try to focus on what I can take care of in the moment. Right now, that means doing my best to graduate with good grades and get accepted to a good college. One day, I hope, I will realize everything I dream of: helping my family out and giving them the life they never had.

But I've come to recognize that no one should expect too much from themselves. Since we are not in control of the future, we should live moment by moment. We should do our best every day we wake up, and see what comes next.

DO FOR YOU

by Shanté Brown

Relax. Read. Do some writing. Take a long walk. Have a good laugh. Do some crying. Pick up a Bible. Reflect on who you are. Envision who you want to be. Pamper yourself. Do what you want to do, for once, instead of doing what is expected of you.

These are all ways to increase your sense of self and gain inner strength.

The important thing is to take some time out for you, to concentrate on you as a person.

Music can help. So can silence. Thinking also works, but sometimes it's best not to think. The important thing is to take some time out for you, to concentrate on you as a person.

Do whatever works for you—for me, writing, music, and aromatherapy are the major things that help me relax and get in touch with myself.

When I get the urge, I just take out my journal and start to write. Some days I freewrite, so I can get all my thoughts across without having to worry about making sense.

Freewriting is my favorite form of writing because I can take all the time I need and write however many pages I want about whatever comes into my head. Whatever is on my mind, getting it out of my head and onto paper is a great stress reliever.

Some days I decide that I am in a poetry mood. This is my next favorite type of writing and for me this comes as a gift. As much as I love to write, I also enjoy being unique, and my poetry is one way that I can satisfy that desire.

Scented candles usually burn as I write (that's where the aromatherapy comes in) and my radio is always on. This relaxes me. Some days, instead of writing, I'll dance in front of my mirror.

Sometimes I just try to get my feelings out. I cry or I try to have a good laugh. This depends on what type of mood I'm in. All of these things help me find peace of mind because they are the things I feel most comfortable doing.

Some days I'll talk to my grandmother, who is now in heaven. Other days I'll say a prayer to God. Sometimes I write down the prayers so I can get a lot more off my mind.

Alone in my room, music playing, candles burning, writing, dancing, or praying, this is for me and no one else. Doing these things, I get a better understanding of myself.

TIPS FROM TEENS ON HOW TO COOL DOWN

130

1.

REBOOT THE SYSTEM

by Adrian Nyxs

I deal with my stress by playing my music as loud as possible. Nothing in the whole wide world is like hearing your favorite song when you need it. Whenever I hear one of those songs, it not only relaxes me, but it gives me that extra boost of energy and endurance for the rest of the day.

When I'm listening to loud music, it drowns out everything else—any stress-causing issues and my thoughts and complaints about the day.

Unfortunately, the loud-music method only works for me in periods of minor stress—when I'm a little annoyed, short-tempered, and tired, maybe because I've just had a long day of school or work or both.

Loud music won't help for major stress periods, those really tough days when I'm too drained and tired to even think. Like when I didn't get

Nothing in the whole wide world is like hearing your favorite song when you need it.

enough sleep the night before, I have both a homework assignment due and a test the next day, and I'm beginning to think my gym teacher is trying to kill me because she's made me exhausted and sore by noon.

After a day like that, I watch TV or sleep it off, almost rebooting myself like a computer. I find that sleeping especially helps, since all the tension is gone by the time I wake up.

2.

PUMP UP THE VOLUME

by Caitlin Lemmo

I used to have an unhealthy habit when I was stressed out or really pissed off: punching things. Nothing was safe from the wrath of Caitlin. I punched a brick wall once and didn't feel it at all because I was so mad.

But now, when I can catch myself as I'm beginning to get stressed out—when I'm somewhere between reaching for a cigarette and punching a wall—I search for music instead.

I'll start singing a song out loud or hum it in my head, any kind of music that I think can help me. It doesn't matter if I'm out in public—if I need to scream, I'll do it. Let people stare. I'll give them a show!

If I'm at home, my preferred method of venting is to sit and wild out to some good music. When I'm really stressed, Nirvana usually comes out of the box. When I feel stupid and stressed, I'll play Nirvana's "Dumb."

Different emotions get different songs. When I feel like there's no hope, I'll put on John Lennon's "Imagine," which asks us to imagine "all the people/ Living life in peace."

When I'm anxious, I'll play some punk like Choking Victim. When I'm lonely, I'll pull out the Beatles's "Eleanor Rigby" with its lyrics, "All the lonely people/ Where do they all come from?"

When I'm mad at a particular guy, feminist rock (rrriot grrrl) is what you'll hear going through my head(phones) or extension cords—perhaps "Rebel Girl" from Bikini Kill. Or any of the Sleater-Kinney songs off *Call the Doctor*.

Allow me for a moment to go old school, and I'll head to my vinyls and put on some Fleetwood Mac—my particular favorite is "The Chain," when they sing "Damn your love/ Damn your lies." So when I don't trust men, I've got the best of all worlds to choose from.

Once in a while, I feel so stressed that I blast my music abnormally loud. Mom calls it devil music, and she'll scream and bang the walls, yelling "Lower that crap!" My favorite part is when she charges into my room and lowers the volume herself—it saves me the effort of having to get up.

Instead of just sitting there surrounded by sound, I often write, which is a big help with my stress. I've had a journal since freshman year. Now I'm a senior, so for a good four years I've had a way of dealing with things.

When I'm mad or upset or feel like reflecting on what I've done,

When I'm mad or upset or feel like reflecting on what I've done, I'll write it down. Sometimes I can churn out 10 or 13 pages in one sitting.

I'll write it down. Sometimes I can churn out 10 or 13 pages in one sitting.

I'm glad I have that journal 'cause I've been able to look back and see my triumphs and tragedies and how I've conquered my disappointments throughout the years.

When my grandfather died this past June, I filled pages on his passing, remembering all the good times we had together. Although my whole family was there for his funeral (31 immediate relatives), I felt as though I had no one to talk to. So to make my pain more tolerable, I wrote it all down.

Last but not least, sometimes when I'm stressed I take a moment to breathe so that I don't react too hastily. I concentrate on my breath: in through the nose and out through the mouth. It's a trick my second-grade teacher taught me, and "in through the nose" has saved my knuckles several times.

3.

WRITE IT OUT
by Kymberly Sheckleford

If I'm really angry or stressed, I find that's when my best ideas come to mind and I begin to write whatever stories come to me. I write fiction and I hope to publish a novel one day. My plots are about love, motivation, or finding strength—sometimes all three. I get a "What if . . . " in my head and then I try to turn it into someone's life.

These stories are pure fantasies and most of my characters are much older than I am, but my work often has a little of my history in it. I find it really satisfying to write about I find it really satisfying to write about characters I can live through. characters I can live through. By overcoming their many problems and obstacles, my protagonists motivate me to go on another day.

> **I find it really satisfying to write about characters I can live through. By overcoming their many problems and obstacles, my protagonists motivate me to go on another day.**

When my life feels like it's spiraling out of control, it's good to know that I can find a sense of peace with a stroke of my pen.

4.

LEARN TO HAVE FUN
by Eric Green

When I'm stressed from school my body feels irritated, and I need to get my troubles out of me physically. I go home to exercise and do sets of push-ups. That helps me calm down and compose myself.

When I'm mad or angry, I feel like a pot of boiling water. Sometimes I take my stress out on my oldest brother David, who's much bigger than I am, by play-fighting—kicking, pushing, and punching him. He said to me one time, "You're strong for a young man," and laughed.

I also play-fight with my older brother William. My brothers don't start up with me—I'm always starting with them.

Play-fighting seems fun at first, but it doesn't always make me feel better. As I've gotten older, I've learned how to handle my stress in other ways.

Sometimes I watch my favorite TV shows. They help me escape my frustrations because I feel better when I'm laughing. Or I listen to one of my favorite radio stations to relax myself and let off steam.

Other times when I'm stressed, I step outside. I go to the library to read books and look up things on the Internet. Or I'll hang out with my friends. And I can always go to a pizza shop and eat a slice.

When I'm at home doing nothing, I relieve my stress by drawing pictures and mixing colors to express myself. Or I take a long nap in my bed and then wake up stress-free. With all these activities, I've been able to control myself and learn to have fun with life.

5.

TALK TO SOMEONE

by Fabio Botarelli

When I first start to feel stressed, I bolt myself in the bathroom to blot out all noise. Taking deep breaths, I give my mind time to unwind so that I lose the temptation to snap at others. I usually remember to bring a bottle of water with me to quench my thirst and fight the urge to devour sweets. If I'm really desperate, I take a shower to vent my stress through my pores. Afterward my mind is usually fresh to do my work and my muscles are no longer knotted.

Dealing with stress often requires the simple pleasure of having someone who will listen.

But if the bathroom treatment doesn't work, my only method for driving stress away is to consult my mom. It may come as a surprise to my fellow teens that I work things out with my parents, but for me, dealing with stress often requires the simple pleasure of having someone who will listen.

Even though I'm 16 and my mom is—well, my mom— she has lived my life before. She was shy and taciturn at my age, with social concerns like mine. When she had a problem, she always sprinted to her mother for help. In a state of stress, I need someone like her to see what's wrong, to help me see the origin of my problem.

One night I came home from a friend's house feeling dispirited. It had been me, Davy, and a bunch of friends from school watching the Super Bowl, and while everyone traded hilarious jokes, I was the silent outcast.

Then it hit me all at once: I was 15 and I'd never dated, I'd never reached a base, and whenever I opened my mouth, I shut it right away. My thoughts that night: "Curse people with social skills, I can't wait till I become rich and powerful so I can hire them as floor-sweepers with just enough money to live."

When I talked to my mom about it, she gave me this advice: "You shouldn't be afraid to say what's on your mind, even if you make a clown of yourself. The gifted socials are not the reason for your fiascoes—your fear is what's holding you back. You think people with social skills are on top of their game, but many are insecure and just want attention." She made me abandon my curse on the socials: I am who I am, and social skills are little things that will come in time.

Stress always has a power source—my mom helps me find it so that I don't have to strike hopelessly at random targets.

6.

EXERCISE TO RELIEVE STRESS

by Nakese Bullock

Research has found that exercise helps people cope better with stress and feel more confident. Some studies have found that people who exercise feel less anxious or depressed than people who don't.

One explanation is that when people exercise, their bodies release endorphins, chemicals that make a person temporarily feel better. Other researchers say that exercise helps the body's central nervous system communicate better with the rest of the body, which can make a person feel better in general.

Some say there's a strong connection between the body and the mind—if you do something good for the body, your mind might also feel more at ease.

Whatever the reason for it, exercising for as little as 20 minutes a day may help a person manage stress and feel better.

It's better to choose an exercise activity that gets the heart pumping faster than normal, like jogging or aerobics, but just walking can help. However, you may not see results right away. It can take a few weeks to start getting the "feel-good" effects of exercise.

GETTING HEALTHY, GETTING HAPPY

by Otis Hampton

We all know that a healthy human being sees a doctor regularly, sleeps enough, eats well, exercises, and avoids drugs and alcohol. But there's more to health than just physical well-being. A healthy person figures out what he or she needs to do to release stress and does it, connects with other people in positive ways, and takes care of those relationships.

We sometimes forget that physical health is very connected to mental health. Stress can cause headaches, irritability, insomnia, overeating, and unhappiness in general. Exercise—things like running, playing sports, dancing, and going to the gym—can help you get rid of stress and have more positive energy. But if you feel angry or tense because of problems at home, school, or work, there are also non-physical outlets to release all that negative tension. When I get bored, I get depressed. A good book (or comic book) often helps me get back into the right mindset.

As many writers know, writing and other ways of expressing yourself creatively are great ways to get out everything you're feeling. I went through a lot in my life before I discovered

I got so bored I decided to help out the little kids. This little girl held my hand and told me I was awesome. I went home that day laughing. It felt good to help out, to connect with the kid, and to get called awesome.

writing as an outlet for all my frustrations. Pick your style: Poetry? Rap lyrics? Stories? Drawing? Dance? Making beats? It's all good because you can use your creativity and make yourself heard without being destructive—or hurting yourself.

It's also important not to isolate yourself. I remember being at a school supplies drive at my foster care agency. I got so bored I decided to help out the little kids. This little girl held my hand and told me I was awesome. I went home that day laughing about it because I'd never heard that from a little kid before. It felt good to help out, to connect with the kid, and to get called awesome.

Many teens try to improve their mood with drugs. Personally, I'm against drugs and drinking of any kind because they're dangerous. I lost my father to smoking, so that holds no appeal. And besides the health risks, getting drunk and high leads to stupid and pointless crap like violence and car accidents.

With your real friends you can talk through whatever's making you upset instead of escaping through drugs or alcohol. Healthy relationships—with family, friends, counselors, or other trusted adults—allow you to say how you feel and not be belittled or intimidated. Everyone deserves respect, and healthy people have learned how to give it, receive it, and feel it for themselves.

We can't control everything in our lives, but there's a surprising amount we can do to feel peaceful, successful, supported, in control, and balanced—you know, healthy.

LET'S TALK ABOUT STRESS

by Caitlin Lemmo and Peter Ramirez

To get advice about stress from a therapist, Peter and I interviewed Dr. Howard Weiss at his office at the Ackerman Institute for the Family, on the Upper East Side of Manhattan. When we arrived, we plopped down on his stereotypical big comfy leather couch. He greeted both of us with smiles. He began with a brief introduction about himself, telling us that he got his Ph.D. in psychology from New York University.

He then asked us, "You guys have any questions?" Peter chimed in: "Do you enjoy your job?"

A smile spread across Dr. Weiss's face—he looked a lot like Jeff Bridges—and he nodded. "Each time I think about it—why I started out in this field—I think about what I'm doing, and how I'm helping people. And, yes, that makes me very happy."

That comment made me believe he is truly genuine. It was reassuring that some people are still determined to make a difference in other people's lives.

—*Caitlin Lemmo*

Q What happens to the body when you're stressed?

A: Our autonomic nervous system responds to stress by turning all systems on. That activation affects various internal organs, muscles, hormones. So when we're stressed, we may experience physical symptoms like headaches, stomach pains, and muscle aches.

When the body stays highly stressed over time, we can see changes in thoughts, feelings, and behaviors. In response to stress, we can become overactive or underactive, and see changes in our sleep cycle and ability to concentrate.

Some people experience insomnia (trouble sleeping), weight loss, overeating, undereating, or excessive drinking (which may lead to alcoholism and damage to internal organs).

Q **What are some healthy ways to deal with stress?**

A: The most important thing is to ask for help. Talking to someone about a stressful event can provide some relief, especially if the conversation results in ideas about how to cope. Among teenagers, that's the biggest problem—finding a way to talk out loud and find solutions to deal with whatever it is that's stressing them out.

Sometimes, people can get so afraid and anxious about not knowing what they're going to do about a situation that they feel even more stressed. Parents, relatives, and friends can be very helpful here. If not them, then seeking help from a professional counselor or therapist can be helpful.

Q **What would you tell kids who feel they can't talk to their parents about certain things that may be stressing them out?**

A: You might feel you can't talk to your parents because you're worried they're going to wig out. But it's usually best when they know the situation. If you tell them more about what's going on in your life, they'll not only trust you more, but they'll also become more rational in their decisions about your life.

If you aren't able to talk with a parent, find a friend or adult who you think will be a responsible listener and who can help you think through the situation. Sometimes, the best help one friend can give another is to put you in contact with someone who is best able to help you with the situation.

The important thing is to connect yourself with others, because otherwise, without someone to talk to, you may be carrying a burden that you don't have to be carrying.

Q **When you were a teenager, were the pressures on teens the same as they are now?**

A: Back in my day (the 1960s), we had a lot of similar modern-day stresses. Yet, because I have a teenage daughter, I do recognize that young people today face many pressures in a more complex world, especially regarding drugs and sex. The media communicates the message in movies and TV that young people should be sexually involved. We didn't feel the same level of pressure when I was a teenager.

Also, academic demands have increased. Getting into some colleges is much more competitive. Teens these days feel that they have to be involved in so many activities, which may increase their exposure to all kinds of difficult stresses.

HOW TO DEAL WITH STRESS

by Jennifer Ramos

What can we do about dealing with the stress in our lives? For some answers, I interviewed Daniel St. Rose, M.S.W., a clinical social worker at Mount Sinai Hospital's Child and Adolescent Psychiatry Outpatient Clinic in New York City.

Q What do you think is the main cause of stress?

A: Generally, environmental demands and internal conflict cause stress. For teens, I think it's a lot about just being a teenager and dealing with parental conflict, sexuality issues, peer relationships, educational expectations, peer pressure, and self-image. Normal adolescence involves issues like separating from parents and wanting more independence, and making decisions about the future. I think for inner-city teens and teens of color, they also deal with racism, poverty, and bad neighborhoods.

Q I've heard that being stressed is a health risk. What exactly are the risks involved?

A: Some of the health risks involved may be physical, like headaches, stomach pains, and muscle aches. Some people suffer from insomnia, poor concentration, poor eating habits, weight loss, overeating, and excessive drinking. Other health risks include heart attacks and ulcers.

Q What do you usually recommend to teens who feel stressed?

A: Take a short break, some time away from the situation, if you can. Get help from someone right away.

Stressed teens should talk to someone they can trust and depend on, whether it's a mentor, a friend who uses good judgment, a parent, a counselor, a teacher, or some other responsible adult. Participate in some kind of activity—an extracurricular club, a sport, running, or other form of exercise.

But also set limits and don't overextend yourself. Be assertive and say no if you can't do something. Pace yourself and use time management wisely. Get some downtime and stay away from drugs, alcohol, and unhealthy foods.

Adolescents need to develop good eating habits. Fast food is unhealthy, as are foods with a lot of saturated fat. You want to eat fruits and vegetables instead of eating a candy bar. It's important for adolescents to have a balanced meal, eat breakfast—things that will help their bodies grow. The body needs the right minerals and vitamins. Being unhealthy in itself is stressful. If your body's not working well, you're going to be more stressed out.

Self-discipline is the key. Stay away from drama! When I say drama, I think that a lot of adolescents tend to protect or have the back of a friend—if there's a fight going on, they want to help out. Adolescents tend to take more risks. They want to get involved in things, and often use poor judgment.

Q **I've been dealing with a lot of stress with my family and schoolwork and often feel like giving up. What kind of advice could you give me?**

A: Certain family situations are very stressful. I think the best way to handle that situation is to talk to someone who you can trust, who you know will support you and be there to listen. Most of the time people need someone to talk to, and that makes them feel better.

If the stress is so bad you're unable to take care of yourself, then you should seek professional help. Talk to someone at school, like a guidance counselor.

The most important thing to do is identify the things that cause you stress. You then need to ask yourself, "How stressed am I?" If you could rate your stress level, using a scale from 1 (least stressed) to 10 (most stressed, cannot cope), where would you be? You need to look at yourself when you're not stressed and compare how you feel.

Usually people who are severely stressed feel anxious, nervous, and can't think clearly. Physical symptoms might include stomachaches, headaches—that's on the "can't cope" scale. If your stress level is severe, I recommend that you speak to a trained therapist. If not, then refer to the recommendations that I mentioned earlier.

STRESS
RELIEF
TECHNIQUES

These techniques are from Carrie Epstein, a clinical social worker and former director of child trauma at Safe Horizon, an organization in New York City that provides support and promotes justice for victims of crime and abuse.

Q What are some techniques teens can use to cope with stress?

A: Thought stopping is what you do if you have a thought going through your head that's stressful or upsetting. Many people feel that we're at the mercy of our thoughts—that if it's in our head we can't do anything about it. But actually, you can.

I talk to young people about picturing a big stop sign and having that pop up, stopping the negative thought. It's one way of teaching that you have control over your thoughts. You can interrupt your own thoughts and refocus yourself. Replace the unwanted thought with something much more calming and less provoking.

I ask young people, "What do you want to replace it with? Is there a safe place you want to think of? Or a calming image?"

You can also do something called "progressive muscle relaxation." Think about a piece of spaghetti that goes from being uncooked to cooked. Or a toy soldier vs. Raggedy Ann. When our muscles are tense and anxious, we feel very tight and stiff. When our muscles are relaxed we feel calmer. You can think about each muscle and let it relax, and that will help you feel calm.

Belly breathing is another technique. Breathe deeply and slowly, so your belly goes out when you breathe in and pushes in as you breathe out. Breathing from the belly can help you calm down.

Q How can talking it out help?

A: One thing that's very important is to help young people identify their feelings. A lot of people of all ages don't know how to say how they feel. They might feel happy or sad, but they might not know the words to explain all the other emotions they're feeling. We help them learn other words: *anxious, confused, helpless, angry*. The better you can convey to others how you're feeling, the more likely it is that other people can respond well.

At Safe Horizon, we tell a story about something happening to a child, and we have the young person talk through how they're reacting to that story. Getting to know the words, having an easier time identifying your feelings, and putting those feelings into words can help decrease stress.

MORE STRESS RELIEF TIPS*

- Take care of yourself: get enough sleep, eat well, and exercise.

- Pay attention to the ways you react to stress.

- Find healthy ways to relax, like talking with supportive people, listening to music, watching movies, taking walks, or doing something creative, like dancing or writing.

- Use formal relaxation techniques like meditation, deep breathing, or thinking positive thoughts.

- Learn your limits—how far you can push yourself and when you need to relax. Learn how to say no.

- Plan ahead, structure your time, and set priorities.

- Ask for help when you need it.

---

*Reprinted with permission from New York Society for the Prevention of Cruelty to Children (NYSPCC.org)

INDEX

A

Abuse
    being caught in circle of, 6
    of mother by father, 38
    reading about, 53
    sexual, 73–74
Academic pressure
    college acceptance, 14
        different requirements of
            colleges, 26
        disinterest in subjects, 26–27
        to good colleges, 27–28, 147
        high school's emphasis on,
            25–26, 45
        parental pressure, 46
    health should be more important,
        48–49
    increase in, 107, 147
Adult responsibilities
    stress from, 1–2, 68
    taking on, 18–21
Albin, Jayme, 79–82
Alcohol, to cope with stress, 100
Anger
    keeping inside, 6, 20
    music to relieve, 133
    sports to relieve, 104, 105
    violence as result of, 7–8, 98
    writing to relieve
        fiction, 134–135
        journal, 133–134
        poetry, 9–11
Anxiety
    as cause of panic attacks, 121–122
    music to relieve, 133
    overthinking as form of, 80
Aromatherapy, 129
Art, as stress reliever, 136
Attitude, focusing on positive, 76,
    124–125, 126
Autonomic nervous system response
    to stress, 144

B

Basketball, as stress reliever, 85–88
Belly breathing, as stress reliever,
    126, 137, 155
Blessings in disguise, 95–96
Body-mind connection
    breathing as stress reliever
        concentrating on, 134
        deep, 126, 137, 154
    exercise and, 139, 141
    physical problems caused by
        stress
        aches and pains, 47, 99, 141,
            144, 149, 151
        colds, 99–100
        fevers, 47
        heart attacks and ulcers, 149
        menstrual cycle dysfunction,
            99
    venting anger with sports, 104, 105
Bravery
    to face stressful situations, 48
    of fictional characters, 54
Breathing as stress reliever
    concentrating on, 134
    deep, 126, 137, 154
Buddhism, 74–76
Bullying in school, 63

C

Calmness, achieved through yoga, 32
Change, can only change self, not
    others, 68–69
Chanting, as stress reliever, 34, 73,
    74–76
Cognitive-behavioral therapy (CBT),
    79–82
College
    balancing present with concerns
        about, 15
    finding right fit, 28

ABOUT YOUTH COMMUNICATION

Youth Communication, founded in 1980, is a nonprofit educational publishing company located in New York City. Its mission is to help marginalized teens develop their full potential through reading and writing, so that they can succeed in school and at work and contribute to their communities.

Youth Communication publishes true stories by teens that are developed in a rigorous writing program. It offers more than 50 books that adults can use to engage reluctant teen readers on an array of topics including peer pressure, school, sex, and relationships. The stories also appear in two award-winning magazines, YCteen and Represent, and on the website (www.youthcomm.org), and are frequently reprinted in popular and professional magazines and textbooks. Youth Communication offers hundreds of lessons, complete leader's guides, and professional development to guide educators in using the stories to help teens improve their academic, social, and emotional skills.

Youth Communication's stories, written by a diverse group of teen writers, are uniquely compelling to peers who do not see their experiences reflected in mainstream reading materials. They motivate teens to read and write, encourage good values, and show teens how to make positive changes in their lives.

You can access many of the stories and sample lessons for free at www.youthcomm.org. For more information on Youth Communication's products and services, contact Loretta Chan at 212-279-0708, x115, or lchan@youthcomm.org.

Youth Communication
224 West 29th Street, 2nd Floor
New York, NY 10001
212-279-0708
www.youthcomm.org

ABOUT
THE EDITOR

Al Desetta has been an editor of Youth Communication's two teen magazines, *Foster Care Youth United* (now known as *Represent*) and *New Youth Connections* (now known as *YCteen*). He was also an instructor in Youth Communication's juvenile prison writing program. In 1991, he became the organization's first director of teacher development, working with high school teachers to help them produce better writers and student publications.

Prior to working at Youth Communication, Al directed environmental education projects in New York City public high schools and worked as a reporter.

He has a master's degree in English from City College of the City University of New York and a bachelor's degree from the State University of New York at Binghamton, and he was a Revson Fellow at Columbia University for the 1990–91 academic year.

He is the editor of many books, including several other Youth Communication anthologies: *The Heart Knows Something Different: Teenage Voices from the Foster Care System, The Struggle to Be Strong,* and *The Courage to Be Yourself.* He is currently a freelance editor.

Real Teen Voices Series

Pressure
True Stories by Teens About Stress

edited by Al Desetta of Youth Communication
Stress hits these teen writers from all angles;
they're feeling the pressure at school, at home, and
in their relationships. The young writers describe
their stress-relief techniques, including exercise,
music, writing, and more. The collection includes
tips for cooling down and inspiring examples of
perseverance. For ages 13 & up.
176 pp.; softcover; 5¼" x 7½"

Rage
True Stories by Teens About Anger

*edited by Laura Longhine of
Youth Communication*
The teen writers in *Rage* have plenty of reasons
to be angry: parental abuse, street violence,
peer pressure, feeling powerless, and more. The
writers give honest advice and talk about their
anger management skills as they struggle to
gain control of their emotions and stop hurting
others—and themselves. For ages 13 & up.
176 pp.; softcover; 5¼" x 7½"

Vicious
True Stories by Teens About Bullying

*edited by Hope Vanderberg of
Youth Communication*
Essays by teens address bullying: physical,
verbal, relational, and cyber. These stories will
appeal to readers because the cruelty and hurt
are unmistakably real—and the reactions of
the writers are sometimes cringe-worthy, often
admirable, and always believable. For ages 13 & up.
176 pp.; softcover; 5¼" x 7½"

Other great books from Free Spirit

The Struggle to Be Strong
True Stories by Teens About Overcoming Tough Times
edited by Al Desetta, M.A., of Youth Communication and Sybil Wolin, Ph.D., of Project Resilience
In 30 first-person accounts, teens tell how they found the resiliency needed to face major life obstacles, live through them, and move forward with courage, confidence, and hope. For ages 13 & up. *192 pp.; softcover; 6" x 9"*

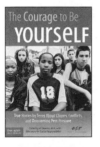

The Courage to Be Yourself
True Stories by Teens About Cliques, Conflicts, and Overcoming Peer Pressure
edited by Al Desetta, M.A., with Educators for Social Responsibility
In 26 first-person stories, real teens write about their lives with searing honesty. They will inspire young readers to reflect on their own lives, work through their problems, and learn who they really are. For ages 13 & up. *160 pp.; softcover; 6" x 9"*

Fighting Invisible Tigers
Stress Management for Teens
(Revised & Updated Third Edition)
by Earl Hipp
Research suggests that adolescents are affected by stress in unique ways that can increase impulsivity and risky behaviors. This book offers proven techniques that teens can use to deal with stressful situations in school, at home, and among friends. For ages 11 & up. *144 pp.; softcover; 2-color; illust.; 6" x 9"*

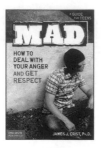

Mad
How to Deal with Your Anger and Get Respect
by James J. Crist, Ph.D.

In this supportive book teens learn whether they have an anger problem, why we get angry, and how anger affects our bodies and relationships. Strategies help them control their anger and avoid poor decisions and actions; insights from real teens let them know they're not alone. For ages 13 & up.
160 pp.; softcover; 2-color; illust.; 6" x 9"

Bookmarked
Teen Essays on Life and Literature from Tolkien to Twilight
edited by Ann Camacho

In 50 compelling essays, young people from a wide range of backgrounds reflect on how words from literature connect with and influence their lives, goals, and personal philosophies. For ages 13 & up.
224 pp.; softcover; 2-color; 6" x 9"

Heart of a Warrior
7 Ancient Secrets to a Great Life
by Jim Langlas

Seven principles, rooted in the long tradition of Taekwondo and tied to courtesy, integrity, perseverance, self-control, indomitable spirit, community service, and love, are explored through a mix of storytelling from the Hwarang and writings from the author's former students. For ages 12 & up.
160 pp.; softcover; 2-color; 6" x 9"

For pricing information, to place an order, or to request a free catalog, contact:

Free Spirit Publishing Inc.
217 Fifth Avenue North • Suite 200 • Minneapolis, MN 55401-1299
toll-free 800.735.7323 • local 612.338.2068 • fax 612.337.5050
help4kids@freespirit.com • www.freespirit.com